M000113228

Praise for

WELLNESS, WELLPLAYED

"Jennifer has introduced me to the miracles that music therapy can perform. She has through her work touched many people in ways that could only be accomplished with both her special gift and her music. Jennifer has shown me with my own eyes what wonders music therapy can perform for people with brain injuries. I've seen the beauty that can arise in the hearts of those who cannot be reached by other types of therapy and yet respond to the magic of music. Thank you Jennifer for giving me and all those that have had the benefit of your work one of the most heartwarming experiences of our lives. May you continue your work and touch the hearts and souls of many souls in the years to come."
DON FELDER, lead guitarist for the Eagles

"Anyone who loves music knows firsthand its therapeutic power, but books like this show how much more we can be doing with music to make ourselves and our communities more whole. Shout out Jennifer Buchanan and the good work of music therapists everywhere!"
SHAD (SHADRACH KABANGO), award-winning rapper and broadcaster

"I would greatly recommend Jennifer's new book *Wellness, Wellplayed*. Not only is it an enjoyable read, her ability to also put a functional framework around the music experience is truly astonishing."
STEVE GILLISS, Guitars for Vets Canada

"For the past 15 years, I have watched in amazement as Jennifer has shared her knowledge, skill, and sheer passion for music and its power to help change lives. The mind and soul can be reached through music in ways otherwise impossible, and Jennifer has allowed so many people to live a more fulfilling life by opening their hearts and letting the music in."
HARVEY COHEN, Vice President, Live Nation Canada, Central Region

"If this great book was a playlist, it would shoot to #1 with a bullet. It deserves a spot on every music lover's bookshelf. Not only is it fun, insightful, and incredibly enlightening, Jennifer has the ability to make you go back and listen to the classics—and newfound tunes, too. It'll give you goosebumps page after page, just like your favorite song."
ERIC ALPER, Freelance Music Publicist, SiriusXM Host

"Jennifer is a fantastic storyteller. She guides us through the importance of music, how our brains respond, and how we can harness its power at different points of the day—to feel energized and connected. The information is truly enlightening. Long live the mixtape!"
GREG BOND, Partner Channel Sales, Microsoft

"Jennifer captures the essence of music for wellness. She shares stories that will make you cry and yearn for the chance to intentionally create meaningful moments using music as a focal point and anchor. For anyone who desires deeper and enriching relationships, follow this book's guidance and you'll be in good hands."
KAT FULTON, Founder, Music Therapy Ed

"Jennifer brings an insight into creating space for music, allowing us to reconnect with our internal values. It gives us the chance to remember with the warmth of experience and the ability to draw us out. This book is necessary, perhaps even on a daily basis."
DOUGLAS MOORE, Business Transformation, Toyota North America

WELLNESS, WELLPLAYED

Wellness, Wellplayed

The Power of a Playlist

JENNIFER BUCHANAN

(((TUNE IN)))
PRESS

Copyright © 2021 by Jennifer Buchanan
All rights reserved. No part of this book may be reproduced, stored in a
retrieval system or transmitted, in any form or by any means, without the
prior written consent of the publisher or a licence from The Canadian
Copyright Licensing Agency (Access Copyright). For a copyright licence,
visit accesscopyright.ca or call toll free to 1-800-893-5777.

Every reasonable effort has been made to contact the copyright holders for
work reproduced in this book.

This book is not intended as a substitute for the medical advice of
physicians. The reader should regularly consult a physician in matters
relating to their health and particularly with respect to any symptoms
that may require diagnosis or medical attention.

Note to readers:
In some instances, people or companies portrayed in this book are illustrative
examples based solely on the author's experiences, but they are not intended
to represent a particular person or organization. Some names and identifying
details have been changed to protect the privacy of individuals.

Cataloguing in publication information is available from
Library and Archives Canada.
ISBN 978-0-9739446-7-9 (paperback)
ISBN 978-0-9739446-8-6 (ebook)

Edited by Scott Steedman
Cover and interior design by Jennifer Lum
Science Consultant: Julie Joyce

jenniferbuchanan.ca

For Mom.
Thank you for loving me and music.

♪

mix·tape
\'mi ks-,tāp\

noun
Traditionally recorded on to a cassette, a mixed tape or mixtape is a compilation of songs from various sources arranged in a specific order.

pur·pose·ful
/pərpəsfəl/

adjective
Something *purposeful* is done on purpose: it's meant to achieve an aim. It is intentional, full of meaning; significant.

well·ness
/'welnəs/

noun
The state of being in good health, especially as an actively pursued goal.

TRACK LISTING

FOREWORD

I HAVE A TIME machine.

It's actually pretty cool. It takes me all over the place. One day it might send me to my childhood home. Another day I might drop in on a friend's wedding from years ago. It's really very good and I use it all the time.

The other day I was telling my friend Terry Stuart about my time machine. Turns out, Terry has a time machine too. His works just like mine—it takes him back and forth between decades, visiting people and places from his past. Terry loves his time machine.

You have a time machine too. We all do.

It's called *music*.

The idea of music as a time machine is not new, of course. We know that certain songs and recordings are very special to us, and those songs can transport us to a different time and place in an instant. We were reminded of this simple idea when we created The Awesome Music Project (AMP), a charitable movement that explores the healing power of music through sharing songs and stories. We created a book filled with stories from people from coast to coast about what songs were important to them and why. And so many of those stories dealt with music as a key to unlocking the past.

Since starting AMP, and creating the book *The Awesome Music Project: Songs of Hope and Happiness*, we have been constantly reminded that our lives have a soundtrack. Our lives are made up of playlists and mixtapes. Curating them, sharing them, and living them is vital to our wellness.

One of the first people we approached for a story about the healing power of music was Jennifer Buchanan. Terry met Jennifer while researching the leading practices of how music can be used to address mental health. He was immediately struck by her passion and dedicated focus to change lives through music. Whether through her music therapy clinical practice, speaking engagements, or books like the one you are reading, she brings the healing power of music to life.

And that is why this book is so important. By developing playlists, we are creating reflections of ourselves and where we've been. It isn't just about the music; it's about what a particular collection of songs and melodies can do to us. And do *for* us.

It turns out that a well-crafted playlist is more than just a pretty cool time machine. As you'll find out through this wonderful book, it can provide comfort and wellness and transport us to a better place.

Here's to making the world a better place, one playlist at a time.

Rob Carli and Terry Stuart

INTRO

Behind Every Favorite Song is an Untold Story

"I don't make music for eyes.
I make music for ears."

ADELE

▶

B ACK WHEN I was in elementary school, I remember hearing the magical call over the intercom: "Please line up, single file, and follow your teacher to the gym for assembly." Assembly, the gathering of all of us together—even the "big kids"—always brought on excitement, curiosity, and anticipation. What was to come next?

On this particular day, there was extra energy in the air, and I noticed my mom sitting on one of the big chairs in the back with my four-year-old sister on her lap. From my vantage point, seated on the floor with the rest of the students in my class, I wondered, "What are my mom and little sister doing here?" I wasn't sure how I felt about that.

In the middle of the gym was a reel-to-reel projector, and at the front was a large screen, a stool, and a single guitar resting in a stand. A guitar? Now, that definitely caught my interest.

Within moments, a cute, older-looking guy walked to the front. Beaming a bright smile, he gave a wave and then said "Hello students!" in a cheerful voice that carried out clearly across the rows.

He then put on a movie—a series of stunning photos of the beautiful West Coast and the Rocky Mountains. As we watched, he shared his message of how to be a good steward of the land and reminded us of the gifts we'd been given. What made his message even more memorable was the fact that, throughout the images and the words, he also added in . . . music.

As he spoke he gently strummed his guitar, adding a dynamic soundtrack to the riveting stories. Imagery, message, and music— all blended together, to become the perfect anchor to a moment I would never forget.

I recognized one of the songs he played that day. I had often heard it coming through the small radio that was always playing in our kitchen at home:

Country roads, take me home,
To the place, I belong...

||

In the auditorium that day I listened, transfixed, as John Denver brought his message to life through music. I may not have recognized his face, nor even his name, but what I do remember was coming away from that day with a long-lasting impression—the prelude to a feeling that would accompany me throughout my life and inform my career as a music therapist. A day that would lead me into seeing others through the auditory lens of music. Learning that behind every note is a deeper story waiting to be uncovered by anyone who takes a moment to listen.

The Power of a Playlist

If I were to try to prepare you for what this book is about, I would simply say that its intention is to teach you how to create a variety of purposeful playlists.

Instinctively, we all know that music is powerful. Music is a gateway into comfort, or total discomfort. It soothes us, it sorts us out, and at times it transports us to a different place. It helps us to remember, and it can help us to forget. Throughout a single day or over the course of a year, music assumes a significant role in cheering us up, bringing down our stress, and helping us feel more secure in the world. Put on the right song at the right time, and you will smile, cry, tap your feet, or just breathe a contented "ah."

Music can best make the impact you need for real change if you get up close and personal to it. The closer we get to something, the clearer our vision becomes. Music, something so familiar and so integrated into our day-to-day culture, is no different. The closer we get, the better we hear.

Soon after re-releasing *Tune In* in 2015, I knew I wanted to give more attention to one of my favorite concepts in the book: designing purposeful playlists. In my thirty years as a music therapist, it has been hands down the best piece of home-health-care-work I have assigned for my clients to do between therapy sessions.

Tune In was all about using music intentionally to reduce stress and boost mood. *Wellness, Wellplayed* is about one specific technique, broken down into several different exercises scattered throughout the book. Each one is designed to give you a process and a product that will benefit your emotional health and well-being. Playlists can be a bridge to something deeper within ourselves, and a way to address our human need to feel, create, and connect.

Perhaps you are asking yourself, "In this day and age of auto-generated playlists and streaming services, what is the point in making my own playlist?" There's a scene in the 2000 movie classic *High Fidelity* that may help answer this question. Rob (played by John Cusack) tells the audience that the meaningful time, dedication, and internal struggle it takes to put together a mixtape is worth the work. "Now, the making of a good compilation tape is a very subtle art," he explains. "Many do's and don'ts. First of all, you're using someone else's poetry to express how you feel. This is a delicate thing."

As you put together such a compilation, you are using someone else's messages to express how YOU feel. As Rob suggests, the process is quite complex. It will give you an opportunity to think about your relationship to music, to other people, and to yourself. You can keep the resulting playlist to yourself, or share what you uncover with others.

The intent of this book is to take you through one, two, or several exercises to help you prepare "Purposeful Playlists" a little bit at a time. This little-by-little approach will help you put in the necessary time and energy without it feeling too daunting. The exercises are not meant to be rushed, but savored and adaptable to your need in the moment.

We are witnessing a major social change throughout the world. Even if we ignore the COVID-19 pandemic (or perhaps because of it), people seem to have awakened to a desire to revisit what they truly value. At the same time, we are using screens more and more, to sort through and make sense of the flood of information. I have heard people compare this time to an emotional hijacking, the likes of which we have never felt before.

In my circle, I have noticed how people are re-examining the power of music in times of change, while researchers and organizations continue to study the role of music in helping people cope, recover, and restore hope.

Uncertain times will always be with us. Perhaps music can be our proven constant.

Use this Guide + Music = Strengthen your Health.

Can music actually improve our health and well-being? The short answer is "YOU BET," and there is so much evidence—scientific, clinical, and personal—that proves it (more about this in Track 2). But how can we maximize what we already know? How can we use music *purposefully*, and how can music effectively and efficiently change the way we think, behave, and believe, at the very time we crave that change the most?

Music, more than ever, can be a sure friend. Even during the most challenging of times, music can reassure us that everything is going to be okay. When you are in transition or feeling lost, it can be the lifeline you need to get you through to the next step—be it a half step or a giant leap. Just like our physical health, our mental health requires attention, perhaps now more than ever. I believe there is no better way to give it the care it needs than through the right music, at the right time, and in the right way.

This book includes the following elements to help you maximize your music:

- Core stories (identified with ▶ and ‖ buttons)

- Exercises (in gray boxes identified with a ♪)

- Evidence—links and sources (included in the "Notes" section at the back of the book)

- Look Through the Wellness, Wellplayed Lens—a music therapist's perspective on the exercises and concepts brought forth in each track.

In theory, putting together a playlist is incredibly simple—but that does not make it easy. This guide will help you dive deep into all the ways playlists can have an impact on your memory, mood, and motivation—the Wellness, Wellplayed way.

wellnesswellplayed.com

TRACK
1

The History of
the Mixtape

"If God is the DJ, then life is
the dance floor; love is the rhythm
and you are the music."

PINK

QUITE SIMPLY, A playlist is a mix of songs.
   Ever since the creation of recording devices and the media to hold a collection of songs in one place, people, particularly young people, have been making playlists. In the 1970s these compilations were best known as *mixtapes*.

▶

During elementary school, and more specifically during my parents' divorce, I discovered the perfect escape from all the noise—music.

My classmates and I spent endless hours recording our favorite music from the radio onto cassette tape. The process was time-consuming. It meant hovering our fingers over a radio cassette player, carefully listening for the announcer's cue that our favorite song was about to come on. The cassette would be in the boom box, ready for us to press the Play and Record buttons simultaneously at precisely the right moment.

You never wanted to miss the opening note. On the rare occasion my thumbs didn't press down at exactly the same time (I used my thumbs because the buttons stuck a little and I could get more leverage), I would have to wait another few hours (or even a day) for the song to repeat so I could ensure it made it onto my playlist.

When we failed to stop the recording at the end of the song, and the announcer's voice accidently intruded, we had to quickly take out the cassette, put a pencil in the left hole, and carefully roll the tape back. That way, the voice would be replaced by music when capturing our next favorite song.

Eventually, our efforts were rewarded with a full cassette of music, free of commercials or DJ patter, to give to our best friend at school the following day. More meaningful than any store-bought gift, the mixtape conveyed affection and respect. It taught us a lesson we would never forget: that music has a wonderful way of showing us what matters.

III

The Evolution of Music Listening and the Birth of the Mixtape

This desire to order our music seems to come from a fundamental human place. It gives us an opportunity to curate what's important to us and highlight our values in the moment and over time. Want a playlist to help your cats relax? It exists. How about a playlist of Sounds for Spacetime Travelers? It's out there. Or try Walk in Like you Own the Place if you feel heavy beats and anthemic lyrics will give you the confidence boost you need walking into your next interview.

DJs have been instrumental in the history of the mixtape. Lexis, a Montreal-based DJ and founder of the music website and collective Music is my Sanctuary, has made the creation of playlists into a career. "I see building playlists, making mixtapes, and DJing as all part of the same ecosystem," he explains. "It's about making junctions and connecting songs and universes that weren't connected before. It's nice to think that maybe you were the only person to make that story."

Long before Lexis, there were DJ icons like Kool Herc, Grandmaster Flash, and Afrika Bambaataa. These legends were recently featured on the docuseries *Hip-Hop Evolution*, a music documentary series that originally aired in 2016 on HBO Canada. Hosted by award-winning rapper and broadcaster Shadrach Kabango (aka Shad), the series tells the history of hip-hop music through interviews with many of the leading cultural figures of the time. Such DJs used mixtapes as demos to highlight their song selection and beat-matching skills, both to sell their work and to showcase the spark they could ignite for house parties and underground community events.

The 1980s, when I was growing up, were the heyday of the mixtape revolution. Mixtapes on cassette became a prominent part of Gen X culture. The mainstream mixtape evolved when personal music devices capable of recording and playing tapes—such as the boom box and the Sony Walkman—elevated the media to an artform among young people. Here was a new way to introduce, experience, share, and popularize music to a large group of your fellow youth.

This period has been so musically revered that the Mixtape Museum (MXM) began to archive, collect, and preserve every example they could, to create a mixtape history. This entire museum is devoted to the art of the mixtape, in loving memory of Orpheus "Justo" Faison, who founded the annual Mixtape Awards in 1995 and was tragically killed in a car accident ten years later. The mission of the MXM is identified on their website: *"Through exhibitions, technology, publications, symposia, collaborative projects, and other partnerships, our aim is to create an environment that encourages dialogue between scholars, music professionals, and enthusiasts on the mixtapes' various functions in society."*

Let's recap this incredible revolution in music history, from the cassette to today's digital streaming lifestyle.

Enter Cassettes

The audio cassette was invented by Lou Ottens. Born in the Netherlands in 1926, Ottens had always tinkered in electronics. During the Nazi occupation in the Second World War, he built a radio for his family to pick up Free Dutch Radio, complete with a directional antenna he called the *Germannenfilter* that could get around the Germans' jamming of the signal. After graduating from university in 1952, he embarked on a long-term career at Philips in Belgium.

To create a music compilation before the introduction of the audio cassette, you needed specialized equipment—typically a reel-to-reel or 8-track recorder—which most people had no access to. When Ottens was promoted to head of Philips' new product development department, he led the development of the company's first portable tape recorder. He was supported in his effort by a team of ten or twelve workers with experience designing gramophones and tape recorders.

Originally, Philips had planned to develop a portable cassette recorder using the RCA tape cartridge system cassette, but Ottens found the dimensions and tape speed unsuitable for their desired portable product. So he decided to develop a proprietary Philips' cassette, with RCA's version as a starting point. He started by cutting a block of wood that fit comfortably into his jacket pocket and walked around to test its security and comfort. This wood block became the template for what would become the first portable cassette recorder.

In 1963, the cassette was introduced to the public. It took some time to be accepted, but once it was, it quickly became the global standard for music production. Contributing to Philips' breakthrough was the fact that they offered this patent and invention free of charge to other manufacturers of similar hardware, such as Sony. Had they not, the compact cassette would never have become the world standard. I wonder what other miracles would happen if other items or processes were not patented but were shared instead?

The cassette equipment invented by Ottens was cheap, portable, and convenient. Each side of the original sixty-minute cassettes would easily fit one side of an LP; the expansion to ninety-minute cassettes allowed for an entire album to be saved on a single side of the cassette. Dubbing between cassette decks unleashed the creation of mixtapes, by which people could curate and exchange their own customized playlists. And once carmakers started installing cassette players in cars, listeners could bypass radio completely and get absorbed in their own creation.

In 2005, a great piece of trivia was shared in Ottens' obituary: Keith Richards from the Rolling Stones used his Philips recorder for making demos. One night, he fell asleep with the recorder on, and awoke the next morning to discover that in between the sounds of his snoring, he had recorded the first version of "(I Can't Get No) Satisfaction." He had no memory of recording it and was forever grateful that Ottens' cassette tape had saved one of rock and roll's greatest songs.

By the end of the '80s, the cassette had begun to disappear, and playlists had a new process for production.

Going Digital with the CD

The first workable digital compact disc (CD) was invented in the late 1960s by the American physicist James Russell. Russell was born in Bremerton, Washington, in 1931. By the age of six he had devised a remote-control battleship with a storage compartment for his lunch.

After earning his bachelor's degree in physics in 1953, Russell went on to work as a physicist for General Electric. He was soon appointed as a "designated problem-solver," and was among the first to use a color TV screen and keyboard as the main interface between computer and user.

Russell, an avid classical music listener, grew frustrated with the wear and tear of his vinyl records. He soon identified that the wear was due to the contact of the stylus on the record—something that could be avoided by using a light to read the music, never physically touching the disk. He recognized that, if he could make the binary code compact enough, he could store not only symphonies but an entire encyclopedia on one disc. "I realized that if I wanted to store music, there weren't enough bits on the conventional digital tape around at the time," Russell said. "So I came up with the optical process."

Through the 1970s, Russell continued to refine the CD-ROM, adapting it to record any form of data. However, like many ideas far ahead of their time, the CD-ROM took years to get to market. The CD as we know it was eventually co-developed by Philips and Sony and released in 1982. Sony launched the first commercial CD player that same year.

The CD's unofficial coming out came with the release of Dire Straits' *Brothers in Arms* album, which was recorded on the latest digital equipment and launched with a tour sponsored by Philips in 1985. By 2007, 200 billion CDs had been sold worldwide.

FUN FACTS

- The first CD was *The Visitors*, a 1982 album by Swedish pop group ABBA

- The biggest-selling CD of all time is the Eagles' *Their Greatest Hits* album from 1976, which sold more than 38 million copies.

In his best-selling memoir *Born a Crime*, Trevor Noah tells a great story about his love of music and how he made a business of pirating CDs. His enterprise really grew upon the gift of a CD burner and a computer. At the time, CD burners were expensive and uncommon, so Noah had a monopoly on the pirated-CD market in South Africa.

Part of what helped Noah's business take off was the fact that he catered to everyone's tastes. He put the personal into the playlist, using only the best tracks off different albums, rather than whole albums. His business partner had another idea: Make the tracks fade in and out so the momentum of the beat wasn't lost between songs. Their party mixes became a hit. Noah did not see this as a crime at the time and asked the question, "If you weren't supposed to download music and burn CDs, why would they make it possible?"

We will look more closely at the issues surrounding piracy in Track 3.

From File Sharing to Streaming

In 1999, just as millennials and the internet itself were coming of age, two young men, Shawn Fanning and Sean Parker, hit the web with a pseudonym and changed the world forever.

It all started around 1998, when someone with the username "Napster" revealed to those present in an internet chatroom that they'd been working on a piece of software that would allow people to dip into each other's hard drives and share their music files.

Allowing a network of global users to easily share music files was a huge hit and the site boomed as the Recording Industry Association of America (RIAA) and other major industry organizations scrambled to catch up (and expressed their displeasure). At its height, Napster hosted around eighty million users. By the time it was eventually shut down in 2001, CD sales were already slowly fading away. Around the same time, the World Wide Web came into being and changed the way we communicate forever.

With the popularization of MP3s (the new compression format for music), the whole mixtape "feel" of writing the names of the tracks on the cassette or CD case cover was lost. The mixtape underwent yet another change, and in the next ten years, digital music curation became the dominant new format. The first music streaming service was launched in 2007, and it was the biggest event in the music space since the creation of the CD.

Buying music from a streaming service is easy and much cheaper than buying vinyl or CDs. And to enjoy a unique mixtape made especially for you, all you need to do is answer a few questions about your preferred type of music or favorite performers. Streaming has become very popular and is how many people choose to listen to music today. It also makes it easy for subscribers to create, share, and update personalized playlists. Access to other people's playlists is a means to stay connected to friends, family, fans, or the public—like Barack Obama's popular summer set.

I just had a flashback. When thinking about how streaming services operate, I can't help but be reminded of my first music subscription service. Several decades ago there was this little club called Columbia House. You would open up a TV guide (the paper, magazine style) and inside would be a fancy pullout that read something like, "Get 12 albums for 1 cent." As a young tween this sounded like a great deal. With your subscription you committed to buying as few as nine albums over the next three years. The cost of future albums were quite steep at the time: twenty-five dollars each plus shipping and handling. The agreement typically ended in one of two ways—you completed your commitment and sent in a physical letter to cancel the subscription, or you received a collection notice due to defunct payments. As with all subscription models, as long as customers experience the value of the product, they'll continue to pay for it. Streaming services seem to have mastered this relationship.

As physical sales and digital downloads declined, music streaming grew with its subscription model. Virtually every song ever recorded was made available at any time in just a few clicks. By 2019, 80 percent of music industry revenue came from streaming and the music industry showed signs of strengthening after its long, CD-declining drought.

There is strong evidence that the songwriters who have poured their heart and soul into bringing their message to the world continue to lose money regardless of the medium used to share music with the masses. Popular musicians such as Garth Brooks and others refuse to release their music on streaming services. As Brooks says, "Songwriters and publishers rely on income from complete albums." Speaking about Taylor Swift and her battle with the major streaming service, he goes on to say, "Songwriters are hurting. So, I applaud Miss Taylor and I applaud everyone for standing up for the songwriters, because without them, music is nothing."

It seems the disparity in revenue between the artist and their record label continues to be wide, regardless of the distribution channel. In the case of streaming this is more easily understood when we learn the two biggest record labels also own the largest streaming service.

Today, complex network servers run algorithms, facilitating the tracking of music plays and royalty fee payments. To some degree, it's still business as usual, and although this book will not be promoting one product or streaming service over another it is important consumers remember that we vote with our dollars. Like almost everything we will discuss in this book, how you choose to purchase and consume your music comes down to personal preferences and values.

Looking Through the Wellness, Wellplayed Lens

It may be just a playlist we're creating, but can we make the world a better place through the process?

The *way* in which we order our music is not as important as *why* we do so. Curating our collections is more than just an exercise—it's also a form of exploration and self-expression. It is an opportunity to reflect upon, and connect to, our internal values and feelings. The echoes of these values and feelings are discernible in the music itself. A playlist opens an opportunity for us to connect more deeply to something within us—and to share with our family, friends, or, even further, the wider community, if we choose to do so.

This concept of a ripple effect reminds me of a business principle and negotiation tactic that has guided me for more than a decade—planning through the lens of a "one-win-everything" model. The Dalai Lama described one-win-everything as meaning everyone wins: you as the owner, me as your customer or employee, your neighbors, your community—the world.

For the ultimate mixtape experience, I believe it is possible to adopt a one-win-everything philosophy. What could that look like, from a purposeful playlist perspective?

- purchase entire albums and support the artists;

- put together personalized playlists for your own listening pleasure and wellness;

- look for opportunities to share and help others through the exercises (*ensure you read the section on "What About Using or Sharing Playlists with Others?" in Track 3 before you do so);

- share music to your community on social media or create a "music hub" (described in Track 5).

Only time will tell how (or if) curated music—the compilation, the mixtape, or the playlist—will evolve and continue. For now, playlists give us an opportunity to be private if we want to be, share if we desire to, and connect with others when we need to feel a sense of belonging. From the legendary DJs to the electronic wizards to the countless music artists out there, there are many of us who are rooting the playlist on.

TRACK
2

The Art and Science of Music

"Music is a language that doesn't speak in particular words. It speaks in emotions, and if it's in the bones, it's in the bones."

KEITH RICHARDS

BRAIN RESEARCH CONTINUES to proceed at an amazing pace, with countless new studies and discoveries appearing every year. I can only imagine this is because we love learning about how complex and amazing our brains really are—and nothing seems to show that off quite as effectively as music.

When I was a kid, there didn't seem to be any rhyme or reason to why I loved the music I loved—my tastes spanned from rock to Broadway, from the music my mom jived to like Bobby Darin to the most current pop hits, and even Kirby Shaw jazz choir arrangements. As I learned to play music myself, I was introduced to more genres and subgenres, from classical to gospel to the latest electronic dance music. Lately, I have been engrossed in both old-school and modern reggae.

I have always been curious about how and why some songs resonate with me more strongly than others—and equally as curious as to why different music evokes the very same emotional responses in others as it does in me. Was it a certain chord progression or groove that drew me in? Did I have a greater affinity to songs written in a certain style? What role did lyrics play in my preferences? (Evidently not much, as indicated by how often my friends would have to say "those aren't the words"!) How heavily was I influenced by the preferences of those friends?

My work as a music therapist deepened this curiosity, encouraging me to stop judging while helping me get to the heart of music and the way it speaks to each and every one of us in a unique way. My career continues to help me see through the barriers that can sometimes keep us apart, arising from our different cultures, races, abilities, and levels of affluence. There is so much we can learn, even the ability to reframe our world view, if we take a moment to listen and open ourselves up to one another's music experiences, tastes, and perspectives.

Science is catching up with what music therapists have been witnessing for many decades—the fact that music can change the way a person feels, thinks, and behaves. Thanks to medical technologies, the public has awakened to the power and potential of using music in almost every health and educational context—and why it's important that we do.

How the Brain Processes Music

For thousands of years, people have sung, performed, and enjoyed music. Researchers have consistently observed that people from all corners of the world listen to or create some type of music, and that all people recognize music when they hear it. While music from various cultures differs in flavor and has a myriad of different meanings and emotions associated with it, every single culture makes music.

Neurologists have long known that there were areas of the brain specifically dedicated to processing music, and with the advent of advanced brain imaging technology, they've discovered that music's reach is far more extensive than previously believed. When we listen to music, sound vibrations in the ear are converted to neural messages and transmitted to the thalamus, the brain's "sensory relay station." After reaching the thalamus, sound information is passed to the auditory cortex and instantaneously broken down into many different elements including, but not limited to, timing, pitch, and timbre (tone). Auditory information is also sent to other parts of the brain to be compared against historical associations and emotional responses (do I like it or not?), stimulating many parts of the brain in both hemispheres.

Although neurologists are still exploring how the auditory cortex functions, they now believe that music processing is much more complex than initially imagined, and involves many more parts of the brain than previously suspected.

When our Amygdala is on Fire

There have been numerous studies on the effects of music on our mental health. We now know that music directly effects the heart of our brain's emotional system—the amygdala.

Just a small collection of cells at the base of the brain spanning both hemispheres, the amygdala is an emotional hotspot. Whenever we see or hear something that makes us feel threatened, the amygdala shifts into gear, and we act before we have time to think. The frontal lobe works in concert with the amygdala, toning down its activity to help us keep our emotions in check and make thoughtful decisions. But when we're stressed, the frontal lobe loses control over the amygdala. When your amygdala is on fire, all you want to do is fight, flee, or freeze (or crawl under the covers with a half-bottle of wine and a bag of chips). It is next to impossible to make a conscious decision—let alone a good decision. In his bestselling book *Emotional Intelligence*, Dan Goleman calls this action an "amygdala hijacking."

But don't fret, music can help stamp out this flame. When you tune in to this wonderful resource (especially music that takes you down memory lane), you begin to activate your hippocampus, where music and memories come alive. When this happens, you experience more feelings of creativity, inspiration, and warmth. As stress declines, your frontal cortex is able to regain control so you can remember what you need to do, tackle a new project with more flexible thinking, and generally feel a level of control you didn't have just minutes before when you were triggered. The best part? You can now make your next, best decision with objectivity and confidence.

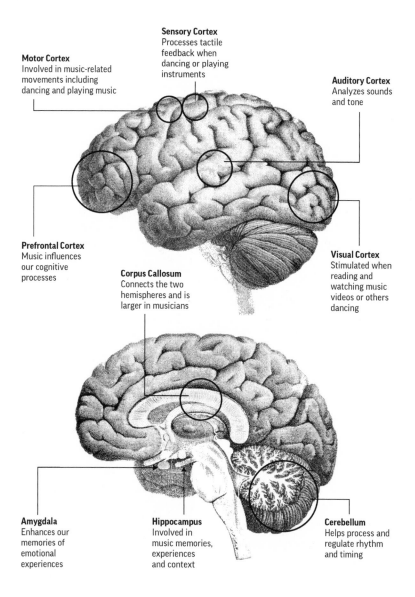

Motor Cortex
Involved in music-related movements including dancing and playing music

Sensory Cortex
Processes tactile feedback when dancing or playing instruments

Auditory Cortex
Analyzes sounds and tone

Prefrontal Cortex
Music influences our cognitive processes

Corpus Callosum
Connects the two hemispheres and is larger in musicians

Visual Cortex
Stimulated when reading and watching music videos or others dancing

Amygdala
Enhances our memories of emotional experiences

Hippocampus
Involved in music memories, experiences and context

Cerebellum
Helps process and regulate rhythm and timing

Music is "Hormonious"

Feeling good feels good. In 1977, Ian Dury released his single "Sex & Drugs & Rock & Roll," a phrase that would be adopted by pop culture for years to come. Sex, drugs, and music all affect the regions of our brain that comprise our "reward system," using the neurotransmitter dopamine to communicate and enhance reward-related memories. With today's onslaught of negative media, opportunities like these to strengthen our synapses for good are certainly beneficial and useful exercises.

I was speaking to a studious-looking MD after a presentation I gave in Saskatchewan, Canada. An avid music lover, he had been sharing the health benefits of music and reasons to socially prescribe it for years. We went on to discuss the benefits of listening to music frequently and intentionally, and the fact that we'd both observed how music helped our patients feel better. He said, "I prescribe medicine to ease the pain, and you treat with music to do the same—they both have tremendous benefit."

Sometimes life can throw you for a loop and what was once manageable becomes difficult or overwhelming. In the field of neuroscience, it is widely acknowledged that emotional and physical well-being are closely intertwined. Emotional distress and chemical imbalance in our brains and bodies are intimately linked. Medications can help to stabilize chemical imbalances and serve an important role in the treatment of mental health disorders. However, it can be challenging to find the right medication balance and mood-stabilizing medications often come with undesirable side effects.

Music can help us tap into our intrinsic mood-stabilization systems that are mediated by hormones and neurotransmitters. As neuroscientist, cognitive psychologist, and best-selling author Daniel Levitin puts it, "The promise here is that music is arguably less expensive than drugs, and it's easier on the body."

Before we look in more detail at four specific hormones and neurotransmitters that music affects, let's do a quick recap on what these chemical messengers do for us in general.

First of all, we know that hormones travel through the bloodstream. Dr. Randi Hutter Epstein, author of *Aroused: The History of Hormones and How They Control Just About Everything*, puts it this way: "Think of them as the body's internal Wi-Fi." Hormones carry messages from the glands where they are produced to cells in different parts of the body. These messages help to "turn on" or "turn off" cellular processes that control, well, essentially everything, including appetite, growth, stress, blood sugar, and sex drive—just to name a few.

The term "hormonal" is usually associated with our mood and the swings it can go through, but in reality hormones play a role in almost every bodily function and can be influenced by external forces—with music as no exception. That is why we can say that, as humans, we are truly hormonious!

Neurotransmitters are another type of chemical messenger. Unlike hormones, which use the bloodstream as a highway, neurotransmitters tend to travel much shorter distances. Their main role is to pass a message from one brain cell or "neuron" to the next. While neurotransmitters themselves do not travel far, they enable messages to be passed across vast brain regions through rapid and extensive neuron communication chains. Like hormones, neurotransmitters play a crucial role in bodily function as well as emotional and mental well-being.

Here are a few key examples.

Dopamine Dopamine is a neurotransmitter that can also act as a hormone, by entering the bloodstream and affecting regions outside the brain. When it comes to listening and interacting with our favorite music, dopamine is known as the "feel-good" neurotransmitter because it stimulates our pleasure receptors and helps us feel more positive about life. These feel-good moments can lead to greater focus and productivity.

Serotonin Serotonin is a neurotransmitter that is important to the regulation of our mood. Music is widely thought to promote mood stabilization by acting on our serotonin system. Dr. Teresa Lesiuk studied music listening for positive mood change (we will be discussing exercises to help this in Track 6). Lesiuk's work validates what many of us have experienced over our lifetimes—listening to music while we work helps us be happier and more creative.

Oxytocin My experience has repeatedly shown that music is effective and very efficient at fostering positive social interactions by promoting trust and cooperation within even the most diverse gathering of people. Dr. Alan Harvey puts it this way: "In a group context, music-related activities...encourage the formation of bigger social networks, help to define cultural identity, and may represent a 'safe-haven' in which individuals can interact and share experiences." In his research from 2020, he goes on to document the links between music and the hormone oxytocin and the influence they have on physical and mental well-being, the key roles they play in bonding and feelings of attachment, and their positive impact on social recognition and social memory.

Cortisol Our levels of cortisol, the stress hormone, have been shown to drop dramatically when we listen to relaxing music. The lower the levels of cortisol, the less stressed or anxious we feel. In patients undergoing surgery, music has been found to be just as effective as anti-anxiety medication at lowering pre-operative anxiety.

The evidence here is quite clear—music acts like a drug. Keeping that in mind, it is important we use it responsibly.

How Does the Science Influence My New Playlist?

So, how does this information apply to those playlists we are going to create? It's not about designing a playlist and shelving it. It's not about creating a playlist for one-time use. It's about creating a playlist that you can incorporate into your life on a regular basis in a meaningful way.

Our emotional response to a selection of music, how that music is administered, and how often we listen to it will all have an effect on us. So, it is important to be aware of our personal musical preferences and triggers, and remember that other people are also just as easily triggered. This includes all the elements of music, from the volume it is played at, the tempo (speed), the specific tones (electric guitar vs. bagpipes), the genre (rap or country), and even the amount of silence it includes. We will continue to delve into the logistics of music listening in Track 3.

At this point, particularly if the information we've covered so far is resonating with you, you may have the feeling you want to delve deeper. You may even want to work through the exercises in this book with professional support. Perhaps you have been struggling more than you realized, or navigating through a difficult transition that you don't seem to be able to rise above. If this is the case, you may want to consider engaging in music therapy. I speak more to this near the end of this track.

Introducing Music to Young Minds

If you currently have young children in your life, let's pause for a moment and reflect on a few important details. From as early as in their mother's womb, there is evidence that babies are aware of and respond to music and other sounds. Mere moments after birth, a baby may turn in the direction of a voice or sound in search of its source. Newborns quickly learn to differentiate their mother's voice from others. There is strong evidence for the connection between stimuli received in early childhood and brain development, so exposing children to music early on can have dramatic and lasting significance for their development and well-being.

When it comes to music, it probably won't come as a surprise to know that when and how children listen, as well as what they listen to, is determined by their unique environment and the people who engage with them.

There is now a lot of data showing the benefits of music on brain development, including improved memory and learning. What I find most interesting is the way music attracts our attention at an early age.

▶

My children were very young when *Barney & Friends* first came on the scene. The program became a staple in our home, largely because it kept them completely transfixed and immobile for the duration of the show, giving me time to do the laundry and get lunch ready.

One day, I stepped away from my own work and decided to do a "mini music case study" to identify what it was about the big purple dinosaur that so enthralled my kids. I found myself sitting on the floor next to my children, stopwatch in hand. My hypothesis? The brains behind Barney had succeeded in pinning down the optimal timing for holding a child's attention, and I wanted to learn what that timing was. I wanted to assess the show's musical triggers, including how often they happened and how much time lapsed in between.

My living-room trial confirmed what I already knew too well: that the show's music was regular, repeatable, and predictable, with a new song starting every 90 to 180 seconds or so and then only lasting 45 seconds to a minute. That made me think about my own early years of television programming with my friends Mr. Dressup, Mr. Rogers, and the gang on Sesame Street. I could see a similar pattern in recalling those shows. We always knew when a song was about to happen, and even though we had heard it countless times before, each time it played we loved it even more. Watching Barney, I found myself moving my head a little and smiling as my children sang along.

❚❚

Along with this premise of creating a regular, repeatable, and predictable means of sharing music with the young people in our lives, I suggest adding diversity. Take advantage of novel playlist titles like "New Music for my Children" or "Brain Activation Music for my Babies" or "Children's Music from Around the World" to find new favorites that can also become a part of your day-to-day listening as your children grow.

Never assume that children are not capable of appreciating a wide variety of music. I am sure you know a child who loves rock and roll, classical, jazz, reggae, world beats, or country music. There is evidence to suggest that our musical preferences start forming before the age of two and, perhaps not surprisingly, most toddlers prefer loud and fast music irrespective of style.

Multicultural music can enhance the moods of children, escalate their acceptance of others, promote harmony and inclusion among children from different cultures, and, most importantly, strengthen their listening skills. Like in all things, we grown-ups have an opportunity, a responsibility, to keep the doors open for our children—exploring diverse music is one of those ways we can make a difference for future generations.

And the benefits of diverse music listening don't stop there. According to Daniel Levitin, discriminate music tastes start at fourteen and peak at twenty-four. While there is a general preference for certain types of music that emerges in young children, they don't yet exhibit distinct preferences at this age.

Just as important as my belief that music should be in every school, is my belief that children should have the opportunity to experience a wide range of musical styles that feature diverse rhythms, instrumentation, and dynamics. The massive array of "world music" is a great place for any young family to explore. Music opens doors, creates bridges, and extends a myopic lens, helping frame our children's world views.

Music Therapy

Although this is not a music therapy book, my career as a certified music therapist drives my perspective, and is the fuel from which the Wellness, Wellplayed point of view and purpose were fully ignited.

One of the reasons more and more people are becoming interested in music therapy is the vast amount of evidence being gathered that proves how deeply music affects us, both psychologically and physiologically. But when we are faced with challenges—rehabilitation, transitions, illness, grief, loss—we need more than music; we need an expert, a witness, a guide, and a counsellor to support and guide us. That is the role of a music therapist.

In 2013, a *Systematic Review of Music Therapy Practice* using medical, psychological, and music therapy databases revealed that people who participated in music therapy programs felt deeper connections and feelings of support when they needed them. Music itself is therapeutic for many, but music therapy takes this connection to the next level to address our clinical and medical needs. Talking is also therapeutic for many, but we need the help of a psychologist to take our perceived brokenness into a place of deep-seated healing and recovery.

Another reason behind the increasing popularity of music therapy is the fact that, as an allied health profession, music therapy can be used in co-treatment with other therapies and treatments—and it does not interfere with medication. There is evidence that music therapy reduces rates of hospitalization and helps to maintain stability and improve psychosocial functioning, and that clients of music therapists suffer less anxiety and depression.

A music therapist's role is to ensure that music is used under the highest of ethical standards and with the largest body of knowledge. Music is a powerful resource that can do great things, but it can also cause harm by bringing up lost or undesired memories at the wrong time. It can strike tones that hurt your ears or take you into a place of agitation. The music therapist is ready with a kit of music resources and a scope of music interventions and counselling skills. They thoughtfully establish a therapeutic relationship, and monitor each person's response to help them achieve their health and wellness goals.

▶

During COVID-19 music therapists had the extra pressures of facilitating sessions virtually or donning complete personal protective equipment (PPE). The heightened stress on all healthcare workers was palpable. As Christmas approached my entire team was looking forward to a short reprieve and rest. Then, on December 24, I received a call asking if I could make a special visit to our city's largest trauma center. I was not given any details over the phone but was asked if I could come within a couple of hours. I was feeling tired but had rarely been asked to spring into action at such short notice. I knew it must be something important.

I got ready, ensured I had all the necessary PPE, packed my instruments, and drove to the center. I entered the large facility and took the elevator to the familiar fourth floor, the Palliative Care Unit. I was met at the door by a nurse and the spiritual care director. They suggested I only needed my guitar and should leave the rest of my kit at the front desk. As we walked quickly to one of the private rooms they explained why I had been called in. A twenty-three-year-old woman was dying and her parents, who had just arrived from India, had asked for the music therapist to help them say goodbye to her. My heart welled up. How could I have anything to offer that could possibly make a difference?

As I waited outside the room, unable to enter as the COVID capacity had been reached, I held my guitar and turned toward the grieving parents. "Wonderful that you are here, we have been looking forward to your arrival," said the mother. "Would you be able to play a slow song for us to dance to? We want her parents happy and dancing to be the last thing our beautiful daughter sees."

As I played "Love Me Tender" the twenty-three-year-old's parents put their arms around one another and moved around the small corners of the room with tears in their eyes. As I watched I thought, it is not always a specific song but the essence of music that can create a new story. It also occurred to me that to the outside world, I must look like someone just singing a song outside a hospital room the day before Christmas. In reality I don't think I have ever had to pay attention and focus so hard. I had to temporarily add an extra therapeutic veil between us so I didn't cry and could provide the moment required.

The song choice took a minute as I knew this couple had just traveled from the other side of the world and we hadn't had time to delve into music preferences. I selected a familiar Elvis tune based on my approximation of the parents' ages and because like Johnny Cash, Bryan Adams, and Shakira, his music reached beyond his own country. I needed to be loud enough from the door that music would fill the room—and I positioned my tone to be as warm as possible. I carefully monitored the tempo to ensure it matched their natural gait and that I repeated it enough times for the twenty-three-year-old to open her eyes a few short moments to see the dream unfurling—music connecting the deep love between them.

▌▌

A music therapy session may have a general framework, but it is never approached by rote. It is conducted in a constant state of improv (musical flux), flowing seamlessly from one movement... one feeling... to another, depending on where the individual needs to go. The therapist constantly monitors the participant's responses to guide them to the next moment and the next step required. Given the nuanced responses people often display, it's a process that takes incredible focus and attention to detail.

All good strategies are best if used with the right intention—music is no different. Sometimes we just need a professional guide.

Countries throughout the world have national music therapy certification programs. To find a professional (registered, licensed, certified) music therapist near you, contact the World Federation of Music Therapy (wfmt.info).

This seems like the perfect time for our first exercise! This one will help us learn more about ourselves, our listening habits, and how often we are musically stimulating our auditory cortex with intention.

Listening to Music

Hearing music and listening to music are two very different activities. Hearing is the physical act of perceiving sounds by the ear. Listening, on the other hand, is done intentionally and requires a certain level of focus or engagement. Purposeful playlists require us to listen.

"Active listening" means that the music is our main focus. The listener interacts with the music in a cognitive, emotional, and significant way, finding the meaning of a song through the lyrics, connecting to the rhythms, and seeking out the repetitive moments and the pauses. Working through the exercises in this book will develop your active listening skills, helping you focus, concentrate, and pay attention.

Our listening habits are the routines and behaviors that add to our auditory diet—such as the times of day we typically turn on the radio or what conditions usually prompt us to turn the music on or off.

My local coffee shop is an integral part of my current listening habits. Nothing makes me happier than great coffee, comfortable seats, a plug for my laptop, and a great mix of "acoustic coffee shop" music to inspire and spark my creativity as I work away on daily tasks. I can count on the music to enhance the bigger experience and would certainly notice if it was absent.

While writing this book, I spent a lot of time assessing my listening habits in my daily life. I was surprised by how little I was taking advantage of music outside of my work. Reading so many articles and books about the benefits of music reminded me of the uniqueness of my music preferences and experiences. Once I started tuning in more regularly, I found opportunities and ways to access and enjoy new music in the car, during some of my more boring admin tasks, as I organized the pantry—and it always came down to a great playlist.

Our music listening habits are unique to each one of us. Fortunately, music is also accessible to most of us, and it's medicine we don't need in high doses to tap into its healing powers. Although the amount of music I listen to varies, I have noticed that its overall impact on me has increased. When I listen to a live performance or plug in my headphones and put on one of my purposeful playlists, I am more often completely engrossed in the experience, and more inspired to continue to add new music to my collection.

Some of my music listening habits include:

- Hearing a song I like and adding it to one of my playlists.

- Clicking on my friend's social media posts where they are sharing a favorite or new piece of music.

- Trying to learn all the words of a new song in my car (and old songs that I continue to mix up the lyrics to).

- Asking my children to play me some of the songs they like.

- Starting with one music docuseries video and then seeing what other videos are suggested.

- Taking time to daydream when a great song comes over the speaker system at a coffee shop.

- If I don't know the song, using an app on my phone to identify it so I can add it to one of my playlists.

- Talking about music memories with my friends.

♪ **ASSESS YOUR LISTENING HABITS**

The simplest way I know of to help you figure out what your current music listening habits are, and to see where a potential playlist can fit, is to ask yourself the following questions. It's a great activity to work through with friends, family, or people at work. Allow yourself to sit back and reflect.

- Where have you listened to music over this past month?
- When do you not listen to music?
- How do you feel when you are not listening to music?
- How are you using music therapeutically in your life right now?
- If you are not using music, why do you think that is?
- If music no longer existed, where and when would you miss it the most?
- How often in a day are you actively paying attention to music?
- Is music continually playing in your home or office? Why do you think that is?

Looking Through the Wellness, Wellplayed Lens

As we continue learning more and more about the power of music to make a difference in the lives of the injured and the weary, let us never lose sight of how music can also impact our day-to-day lives. This is undoubtedly where creating and using purposeful playlists can make a significant contribution.

The science behind music therapy, music and medicine, and music and health and well-being is becoming well documented, but it is also most certainly just the tip of the information iceberg. Much more will be revealed over time.

Research is good, but the ways in which it can be translated to help change the way someone lives for the better is golden.

TRACK
3

Set Yourself (and Others) Up For Success

"I think music in itself is healing. It's an explosive expression of humanity. It's something we are all touched by. No matter what culture we're from, everyone loves music."

BILLY JOEL

BEFORE WE GET into discussing the best sound source and the logistics required to get the most out of your playlist experience, let's start with a simple question. How would you describe your music using just three words?

> ♪ **JUST THREE WORDS**
>
> Think about all the music you've been listening to lately—the music you have been particularly drawn to, whether on the radio in your car, or at the coffee shop, or through a streaming platform, or on your personal stereo. Imagine all the music in your life right now, and then consider the best three words to describe it. The music you listen to when you jog, the music that's playing the most at home—how would you describe it in just three simple words?
>
> Is your music strong, soft, exciting, calm, charismatic, busy, high-energy, relaxing, edgy, fun, thoughtful, dark, light, happy, sad, inspiring, deep, confusing, harsh, bright, political, folksy, energetic, dreary, light, quirky, upbeat, joyful, soothing?

Choose three words that seem to best describe your music. Only three. Write those three words down, or just repeat them to yourself in your mind.

_____ — _____ — _____

Look again at your three words and say them to yourself one more time—the three words that describe the music you have been listening to the most.

Now here's the follow-up question...

Since you are so closely connected to the music you listen to and you understand your music, especially the music you feel drawn to that is so incredibly personal to you, might it not make sense that perhaps, just perhaps...

...those same three words also describe you?

Think about that for a minute. Think about the three words and whether there is any connection to how you would describe yourself.

If Yes, rest in those words for a while.

If No, is it possible that those three words represent the qualities you aspire to?

I wanted to examine our current music listening preferences at the beginning of this track because I want to continue looking more closely at our music and the personal insights it reveals.

In tracks 5, 6, and 7 we will look at specific playlists that strengthen memory, mood, and motivation. But like in all things, before we embark on too many more exercises it is important to put in some time to consider what we will need to feel successful throughout the process.

PLANNING FOR SUCCESS

To be truly successful at developing a purposeful playlist, there are four critical steps to follow:

1 Identify your desired outcomes (goals, aims, targets, focus);

2 Put together the right toolkit for your needs (what you will be using to create the playlist itself: computer, phone, sound source);

3 Select the right music (it will be easiest if your music is accessible in digital format);

4 Do the exercises throughout this book, perhaps with a partner to share them with.

1. Identify Your Desired Outcomes for Your Purposeful Playlists

Whether you are building a house or a playlist, it's all about having a good plan and the right resources. The best chance of success starts with knowing your "why?"

I know that some readers will lose interest right about here. Goals are old-school and they don't work, right? I completely understand this mindset, and ask that you bear with me for a moment as I explain *why* you need a why. For music to be most effective, knowing your why will help you approach each exercise with the right focus and ensure you receive the desired benefits at the end.

I recognize you may have several whys for using music—to de-stress, to boost your memory, to increase your productivity, to lessen your anxiety. Whatever your objective may be, just naming it will help. In her book *The Success–Energy Equation*, Michelle Cederberg puts it this way: "When you set a goal, your attention is naturally drawn toward what you should do next. Your brain starts to look for ways to accomplish that goal and you gain focus, which is an antidote to all the distractions and low-priority tasks that compete for your attention every day." Cederberg goes on to discuss goals in the most beautiful and musical way: "If your goals don't resonate with you at a deeper level it will be hard to stay connected to them."

NAMING YOUR PLAYLIST GOALS

So why do you need a purpose playlist? Here are some of the most popular goals I have heard from family, friends, and clients:

- For comfort
- To reduce stress
- To lessen anxiety
- To improve mood
- To find purpose
- To increase productivity
- To boost creativity
- To feel inspired
- To strengthen relationships
- For general self-care

Take a moment to reflect upon one or more overarching goals you have in your life. Big goals help us expand our vision and stay open to possibilities. This mindset will help us move through the exercises seeking sustainable benefits.

Keep in mind that the exercises in this book are meant for personal use. If at any time difficult memories or feelings arise, or if perhaps you have received a clinical diagnosis, then I recommend working with a healthcare professional to be sure to have a successful and safe experience. Music therapists, social workers, and mental health therapists would all be a great choice.

2. Put Together the Right Toolkit for Your Needs

I'm no stranger to physical media. I had a Sony Walkman when I was a kid. I remember the 8-track in our Cortina, the cassette player in the Oldsmobile, the eventual progression to a CD player, then a multi-CD player in my Honda CRV, and then finally Bluetooth in my new SUV. I physically "touch" music when I play my vinyl collection in my living room, when my hand drives my mouse through the collection of music on my desktop, and as my index finger scrolls through the playlists on my phone. I've gone down the rabbit hole of streaming services, where I've found myself picking a random playlist and streaming an endless river of tunes as I work from home.

The first step in creating your playlist is to put together the right toolkit. Your resources will be uniquely personalized according to your preferences, your needs, and what you are able to access. When we exercise, we change into a pair of running shoes and a comfortable shirt and shorts so we can move in the way we need to move. Like our running gear, our music equipment does not have to be complicated, but we do need certain elements to ensure the exercise is successful.

Here are some examples of what to look for when you purchase, borrow, thrift, donate, and share music resources as you build your unique toolkit. I have purposefully excluded specific brand names as these will continue to evolve and change. Finding the most appealing and affordable resources for you is part of the fun. There is a lot out there and I will share tips along the way on how to explore and find exactly what you need.

How Will I Listen to My Music? The first consideration before we look at making the playlist is how we will hear it—the actual headphones or speaker(s) we will use. Whenever I am asked about where money is best spent in pursuit of a great music experience, "a quality sound source" is always my reply.

For an average listener, sound quality is usually a measure of enjoyability. There is no absolute reference for sound quality; it's entirely a matter of personal taste. Enjoyability is also totally subjective. Every person has their own opinion and preference as to what constitutes good sound quality. Some people really don't mind that old stereo Mom bought at Woolworths forty years ago; others can only really enjoy a song on their expensive European-made speakers.

When it comes to headphones, a lot of people like deep, strong bass, but some prefer a more natural sound. It can also depend on the type of use. If you are into fitness or sports, you might be interested in headphones that will work best during high activity (bulky headsets need not apply).

Regardless, when listening through headphones, earphones, or speakers, you alone can and should decide if something sounds high-quality to you. Keep testing and asking questions.

In my work with the Canadian Hard of Hearing Association (CHHA), we delved into what kinds of sound sources are best for those who are deaf or hard of hearing, and we also discussed protection for the hearing we have. High-volume, risk-associated behaviors can permanently damage hearing capacity. If you can hear someone's music through their headphones when you are sitting beside them, it can mean one of two things. Yes, one is that it is way too loud. But two, it may just be due to a really poor-quality set of headphones. When I was talking to CHHA, I learned that the better the sound quality, the less people tend to turn up the volume. Preserving our hearing is a part of preserving our overall health, so consider investing in a good pair of headphones.

3. My Music: What Will I Use to Make My Playlist?

I have heard there are people who firmly believe the original cassette will eventually make a comeback. However, there is no doubt that digital music and streaming will continue to be the primary access point to our music for some time to come. Recent innovations have led to the development of an ever-growing collection of music apps and technology platforms, many of which ask subscribers a series of questions about their favorite music genres and artists to help them work out what songs might appeal to their tastes.

You may not feel you need this kind of guidance as you read this book and immerse yourself in the Wellness, Wellplayed mindset, choosing music with the express purpose of making your own purposeful playlists for health and other benefits. However, having new songs suggested for you based on your answers to a few simple questions is a fantastic way to discover new music that you may never have known about otherwise—and that you'll enjoy listening to enough to want to add to your personal soundtrack.

PROS AND CONS OF STREAMING

If anything, streaming makes it impossible to ignore just how important music customization has become. Of course, there are pros and cons to streaming:

Pros:

- Streaming gives subscribers ready access to a vast range of music—30,000,000 songs and counting.

- Streamed music can be enjoyed almost anywhere.

- The sound quality of streamed music is superior to that of CD-recorded songs (and infinitely better than the cassette!).

- Subscribers can get nostalgic and listen to recordings from a bygone era.

- Streaming doesn't take up space on the listener's hard drive.

- Personal playlists are easy to create and share with others.

Cons:

- Purchasing music is less of an "event" than it once was. We are missing the artistic element of CD sleeves, album covers, inserts, and colored vinyl.

- Subscribers typically don't own a copy of the music they've streamed.

- Big corporations and tech companies benefit the most (see my comments on "ownership" near the end of this track).

- Most artists are not receiving fair compensation for their work.

- Many music streaming services collect and store user information and don't take privacy seriously.

- Most music streaming services display and depend on ads to stay viable.

- The technology takes time to adapt to and many elders who have not yet learned how to stream are being left out of the transition.

What About Using or Sharing Playlists with Others?

One of the most time-consuming (but, arguably, most rewarding) ways to help those who do not have access to the tools they require is to share your time and resources to work with them.

Using and sharing playlists with others is an opportunity to learn about one another. It is about creating connections, staying curious about others, and listening to what is important to them. You may have the tools, and they may have the stories. Together both of your lives will be enriched.

Learning about someone else's personal soundtrack can be nothing short of transformational but it is a process that requires time and careful consideration. This is especially true for those who are unable to verbally articulate their musical preferences. Although asking family members and close friends may be helpful in this regard, there are multiple factors to be considered. There have been many stories in the media highlighting the relationship music can forge between people of all ages and abilities. It looks simple enough but as we are learning throughout this book, there is additional information that will ensure the success of the experience for all parties.

Dr. Laurel Young, a music therapist researcher at Concordia University in Montreal, Canada, critiques the oversimplified portrayal of music as a nonpharmacological "magic pill" to be "prescribed" to people living with dementia:

> Although neuroscience research helps us to understand cognitive processes underlying music, individuals' musical experiences, cultural backgrounds, and personalities influence *how* they respond. Music that I perceive as happy or pleasurable may be experienced very differently by others. We also cannot assume the music you wanted to hear yesterday will be the same music you want to hear today. If music becomes irritating or overwhelming, it needs to be turned off or changed immediately. If it evokes strong emotions, whether happy or sad, someone should be there to provide support. Music must always be used with care and genuine understanding of each listener's current needs and preferences. When this happens, music may serve as a bridge via which persons living with dementia feel connected to their sense of self, their environment, and others.

There are many human needs—food, shelter, fresh water, loving relationships, ways to contribute, just to name a few. Would it go too far to suggest music be added to the list? At the end of this track we will continue the conversation about sharing and ensuring everyone has access to music and the tools required to benefit from the power of a playlist.

Music Ownership

Whenever possible, *pay for your music!* That is my overarching message with regards to ownership. Purchase full albums as often as possible. Follow your favorite artists and be open to new artists that may not be mainstream-popular—yet.

Piracy became a major problem in the '70s and '80s and caused a number of issues in the music industry. Although DJs popularized the use of mixtapes, the fact that many of them contained copyrighted material made them illegal. To release a mixtape legally, a DJ had to get the individual rights to sell every song included on it.

In early 2021, an incredible list of artists wrote a letter to the British prime minister. Signed "on behalf of today's generation of artists, musicians and songwriters here in the UK," the letter requested that UK law be updated to "put the value of music back where it belongs—in the hands of music makers." It went on to stress that "only two words need to change in the 1988 Copyright, Designs and Patents Act...so that today's performers receive a share of revenues, just like they enjoy from radio play." A committee of MPs agreed, submitting a report that said the music industry is weighted against artists, with even successful artists making "pitiful returns" from streaming. They called for a "complete reset" of the market so that musicians receive a "fair share" of the millions in revenue record labels earn from streaming.

Our Auditory Diet

As we continue to identify the tools and resources we need to fully bring recorded music in a meaningful way to every person who seeks it, it's important that we step away from technology and get a little closer to our natural environment.

Let's engage our auditory cortex...and explore our natural playlist.

♪ CHARTING YOUR AUDITORY DIET

You may not find tables to be all that exciting, but they are highly effective tools for framing a concept; in this case, to get you thinking more deeply about the sounds in your environment. This one consists of a column for feelings, another for "sound at home," and a third for "sound at work." Let's get busy...

AUDITORY DIET		
Feeling	Sound at Home	Sound at Work

In the left-hand column, list four feelings that you typically experience each week. Boredom? Joy? Frustration? Lethargy? Once you have that column filled in, think about the sounds in your home or work environment that consistently seem to trigger that specific feeling. An example would be the feeling "soothed," and a sound you often hear at home that always makes you feel that way might be when your dog is quietly snoring.

In our day-to-day existence, we tend to put so much emphasis on the visual—what we see—but don't place as much weight or value on the auditory—what we hear. This exercise can help us build stronger connections between our feelings and our entire sound world. It can also remind us to appreciate nature's playlist—one that requires no technology whatsoever.

Going Old-School

A few years ago, I re-invested in a record player. It was time to bring vinyl back into my life. The growing popularity of streaming meant that I'd forgotten the pleasure of listening to and appreciating albums in their entirety, and I'd noticed that there were fewer and fewer new albums being released. So I bought a record player.

It looks like I started a trend because in 2020 vinyl record sales surpassed CD sales for the first time in a generation. And although I would have thought it was other Gen Xers like me who were at the forefront of the resurgence, surveys show it's in fact millennial consumers driving the vinyl revival.

I don't know if you've yet taken this step yourself, but if you haven't, I highly recommend it, regardless of your age. It is so fun and fulfilling to replay old albums, and even new albums. Visiting one of the few musty record stores left in the east corner of my city brought up long-forgotten memories that sparked my curiosity and rekindled my joy. I went in search of my favorite albums, suspecting they would be long forgotten, the last copies sadly sold, and was thrilled whenever I was able to find them again. It felt like the best of both worlds—revisiting the past and bringing it back into the present.

Having a record player again also reminded me of the real impact and importance of this most significant form of the playlist that has largely gone by the wayside—the complete album. The entire album, consisting of an incredible, often interconnected playlist, represents the artist's message and is a powerful form of expression. And so, I've started interpreting each album as a story the artist is telling me, the feelings they wanted to share with me.

My new purchases gave me a great opportunity to share this approach on social media. Even today, if you search #jens10 on Facebook, this is going to come up. What I set out to do with #jens10 was to call attention to the "core" albums. The list did not so much consist of the albums I listened to the most as the ones that impacted me the most at the time. From there, I was able to curate the list down to just ten significant albums that had made an indelible impression on me over my entire lifetime.

♪ **#YOUR10 ALBUMS**

So, here I am looking at my top 10 albums. Complete albums. Not a collection of individual songs but the entire A and B side (and sometimes there was even a second album). As I listened, stories from decades past and the home I grew up in came flooding back. I felt my feet resting on the back of the couch as I read, the music my companion in the background. My feathered hair, favorite plaid pants, and the long drive with my family to a campsite. I remembered my mom working tirelessly in the garden, and going to visit the neighbors with the Firebird in their front yard—the place where I was first introduced to Van Morrison, Peter Gabriel, and the Eagles *Greatest Hits*.

I was certain others shared these same memories, and because my social media feed most days already consisted of music and stories, I felt this would be a great fit for my followers. I started a series, releasing an album once a week like it was the first time ever it had been shared with the world. Each post was accompanied by music trivia of some sort, and a description of the personal significance of the album for me.

So sit down and ask yourself, what is #Your10? You do not have to be concerned about the sharable factor of your personal list. #Your10 can be private, just for you to savor alone. Or perhaps it's a concept you can introduce at your next gathering with family or friends, inspiring a discussion around the dinner table about the top 10 albums that have shaped their lives.

For me, this felt like an inspiring and positive exercise to contribute to social media. You can still find my #jens10 hashtag out there in cyberspace if you put it in the search. I'm curious… what is your #Your10 going to look like? Send me a note through social media—I would love to hear about it!

You can reach me at:
Twitter: @musictherapy
LinkedIn: jenniferbuchananinc
Instagram: @jenniferbuchanan.mta
#wellnesswellplayed
#powerofaplaylist

Looking Through the Wellness, Wellplayed Lens

Not everyone can carry their music with them all the time, even though many of us choose to do so because we have some or all of our music on our phone or other small personal listening device that we can take wherever we go. The modern convenience so many of us take for granted is still not a possibility for everyone. Music has a diverse audience.

In the interests of creating an equitable playing field so everyone can enjoy music equally, I encourage every reader to be mindful of differences in preferences, cultures, and levels of accessibility. Just because we have access does not mean everyone does. It is easy to forget that many people have little or no Wi-Fi service, for example. And althought the pandemic seems to have accelerated governments addressing the "digital divide," the new policies, regulation, and infrastructure will take time.

Dr. Cynthia Bruce, a blind activist, researcher, and educator speaks to this in an article on ableism. Ableism is defined as discrimination against people with disabilities and it expresses when those with disabilities are not able to have equal access. In the busy-ness of our everyday existence, many of us fail to notice the countless small ways in which ableism manifests itself. We become resigned to inaccessible buildings, and to the lack of Braille, electronic materials, and screen-reader-accessible web applications. We are unsurprised by public spaces that are impossible for all to navigate because they are in poor condition or have been designed without consideration for accessibility.

And then there is the cost. Sure, there is still radio and free live music, but the essence of the playlist requires personal control during the creation process. For this we need equipment. Today's tools don't come cheap. Here are some simple yet effective things you can do to help those who may lack the basic resources for building a playlist.

Donate, Fundraise or Volunteer your Time

One of the quickest and most obvious ways to care for others is by donating directly to a charity that works to helps people or groups in need (e.g., elders in care, schools, persons with disabilities, low-income families) to purchase or access the technology to bring music into their days. Able to do more? Host a fundraising venture in partnership with a local charity to raise funds. Vote with your dollars. This can take the form of procuring your resources from companies and organizations that donate a portion of their proceeds to charities that work to ensure everyone has access to the necessary technology and resources, like quality Wi-Fi, tablets, personal listening devices, headphones, or subscriptions to streaming services.

Inform Yourself and Raise Awareness

One of the simplest ways to help others is to stay informed on the issues. You may be unaware that poverty has become more prevalent in the past few years. This leads to limited access due to lack of income and other barriers. Pay attention to what is happening to others in your community—urban and rural. Seek out ways to increase access to technology and reliable Wi-Fi for marginalized groups. Build buzz and connect with local government officials and regulating bodies for telecommunications. The message you need to communicate is simple and goes something like this: "My name is _____, I live in _____, and I want to demand/ensure access to Wi-Fi and other necessary technologies for citizens who don't have access to it." The job of our officials is to help us find a way. You may need to send several requests.

If you are feeling too old for all this new technology, or you are having a hard time keeping up with it all, I get it. If you struggle to access your music or to upload songs onto a personal listening device, or even if you don't own one yet, there is a great solution—ask for help. I assure you, you are not alone. I meet many people who for some reason or another are not equipped to put together a playlist. If this is you, I highly recommend adopting the one win–everything perspective. Find a person in your life who would benefit as much from learning about your music and stories as you stand to gain from their help in learning about music technologies. Together, we all win.

TRACK
4

Your Personal Soundtrack

"No matter what these people say about me, my music doesn't glorify any image. My music is spiritual when you listen to it. It's all about emotion, I tell my innermost, darkest secrets."

TUPAC SHAKUR

WHEN PROMPTED TO remember your favorite song from high school, you may recall not only the song but also your friends, your school, the park you hung out at, or the couch in your friend's basement where you listened to endless repeats. When you think of songs from that time in your life, what feelings come to the surface?

It's long been known that music triggers powerful recollections, but now a brain-scan study has shown us even more. The part of the brain known as the medial pre-frontal cortex sits just behind the forehead and helps us travel down memory lane. "What seems to happen is that a piece of familiar music serves as a soundtrack for a mental movie that starts playing in our head," suggests Petr Janata, a cognitive neuroscientist at the University of California, Davis.

▶

As I sit with Carol, we begin to unpack her desired goal. Research suggests that most people stop adding new music to their personal soundtrack after the age of thirty. At fifty, Carol didn't want to become a part of that statistic, and had sought my support in learning how to explore new music that would help her feel the way she wanted to feel.

We started by reviewing her previous music experiences—her personal soundtrack —to better hone in on how she wanted to feel. We specifically addressed her key music memories, from early childhood to today. This took several sessions to document because, as expected, many stories bubbled to the surface as soon as the memory was accessed. Memories of her high-school sweetheart, her first husband's loud and raucous music, her daughter quietly listening to classical music while studying, and the many moments she stopped listening to sound and preferred nature's stillness as her track of choice. Throughout those stories were woven themes and feelings that she had slowly forgotten about.

As Carol grew older, she had listened to music less and less. Work had its demands and consumed her focus. Her feelings of pressure increased after she'd recently succeeded in landing a dream promotion to head of operations at her advertising firm. She felt guilty about entertaining any negative feelings at all when her career was doing so well. She was grateful for the work and did all she could to keep up with the perceived demands of the job. Yet at the end of each day, she felt like there was a vice around her chest and would pour herself a healthy glass of wine. The visible stress around her eyes, her admission to having difficulties with sleep, and the frequent spats she was having with her new partner served as further evidence that her health and well-being were at risk. She desired a change—not in her job per se, but in her feelings toward her job. As we traveled through her soundtrack, we uncovered the forgotten sides of Carol that she was no longer exploring or strengthening—the epitome of feeling off-balance.

Over the course of several sessions, Carol shared her life experiences and feelings of perfectionism, "loneliness at the top," and lack of connection to others. She was worried these feelings were going to affect her new relationship. She finished her personal soundtrack and with encouragement circled all the times she'd felt the positive vibes she craved—when she had fun, or felt love, or felt inspired, or learned something new…even when she felt challenged. She started to play music more frequently and even brought the guitar that she had loved to play in high school up from the basement. She began to notice herself humming as she moved around her home.

The next step was to add in new music that would inspire the state(s) Carol wanted to pursue. Music that she could put on at any time of the day to begin to anchor her desired emotional state to her new dream work and personal life.

We identified the fact that her work was only one aspect of who she was becoming. When we have a singular focus like work and fall out of balance, music has the capacity to strengthen our creativity and reveal another side to our personality. Carol didn't have to give up anything, just add something in. She was ready to defy the research odds and add in new music post-thirty...to help her explore what it meant to live her best life.

▌▌

Now it's your turn. Let's work through the baseline of your listening...the mother of your music...the ultimate mixtape—your very own life's soundtrack.

If this exercise feels too daunting in the moment, no worries. Each section of *Wellness, Wellplayed* works just as effectively as a stand-alone. Move around, explore, dig into small chunks as and when you feel the need. Just like music, this book has no rules or obligations. Whenever you are ready, your life's soundtrack will be waiting for you.

♪ BUILD YOUR LIFE'S SOUNDTRACK

You'll create your life's soundtrack by selecting those songs from your music library—consisting of all the music you have encountered throughout your lifetime—that represent key events and memories. Creating our life's soundtrack offers us a glimpse into how our music choices over many decades affect us, and how the music of our life and the stories we associate with it have molded us. Specific songs or even styles of music can eventually become your anchor songs, songs that tie you to a particular feeling, so that when you hear that specific piece you feel rooted into that same emotional state time and time again—anchoring the strong, vibrant feelings you need in your day-to-day life.

The first step to begin working on your personal soundtrack is to sit back and let your mind wander and wash over some of the music that has crept in or landed hard throughout your lifetime. Even if you do not write anything down today, get your mind activated on the music that you've been influenced by since you were young.

With a piece of paper by your side or on your computer, construct the following chart.

Each category may have its own page (or several). You may feel most comfortable working on a screen or in a journal. The process is as personal as the exercise itself.

Think of your earliest musical memories, i.e., the music you enjoyed while you were at elementary school, junior high, high school, when you were a teenager, a young adult, and right up until today. As you go through each phase, remember to make notes about those memories in the side column. For each segment, make it a goal to list from three to ten songs, genres, bands, and memories.

Age	What music are you listening to at this time?	What are your associated memories?
Earliest Music Memories: Birth to Grade School		
Grade School		
Teen Years		
Adulthood		
Today		

Essentially, that's it! But remember... just because it seems *simple* doesn't mean it will be *easy*, which is why I have written the rest of this track to support you along the way.

As you make a list of music for each of the stages of your life, chances are you'll begin to remember specific artists, albums, and songs you had completely forgotten about. Take a moment to let those memories develop. This is not about making a list of your favorite songs; it's about making a list of musically inspired moments and memories that mean something important to you.

Earliest Musical Memories: Birth to Grade School

The first category is the music from your earliest years. Some of you may remember a lot of the music or other sounds you were exposed to at this time: the opening of a jewelry box with a music dancer, the game *Operation* with its pings and pops, a scratchy record player in the corner of the living room, toys that played a repetitive tune as you pushed them along, a doll that shared so many different sounds. Others may remember very little from this time in their life. This is not uncommon, and I don't want you to worry about the quantity of sounds or songs you do remember. Just document whatever you can and take a moment to feel it.

If you can identify some of the music from these early years, do you still listen to any of it today? Perhaps you still turn to some of these tunes—the lullaby a parent or family member sang to you when you were a baby—to help soothe you.

I personally can recall very few music memories prior to school, but I do remember many sounds. I grew up in a '70s suburban town. The familiar sights and sounds of the time were typically mothers hollering for their children who were playing nine houses away, lawnmowers sputtering and rumbling along as they attacked each blade of grass, children riding their bikes in the middle of the road while ringing their bells and shouting, dogs barking and howling at other dogs as they encroached on their territory, and the occasional radio blasting from a shiny new Camero or Firebird. These sounds are as vivid to me now as they were when I was eight years old. This was my neighborhood music, and I love it whenever I hear those same sounds now, wherever I am. It makes me feel warm and loved, just as I did when I was a kid.

Your turn. Think about your earliest music memories and add the details into your personal soundtrack.

Grade School

Grade school is a time when group music is introduced to many children, and we may or may not be listening to the radio or songs on TV shows. It is also when many of us first experience the opportunity to sing in a choir, play in a band, or just share music we have come to love.

I experienced my first "live" music performance in grade two. Half a school year had passed before Mr. Trudea walked into our class with a guitar case in hand. I had never witnessed a music teacher making music before with just their voice and a guitar.

Like our regular teacher, Mr. Trudea sat on the piano bench but, instead of facing the keyboard, he turned to face the entire class. We were all huddled together on the carpet, looking straight up at him expectantly. He began to strum and sing with a clear voice, allowing us to absorb every word. I was in awe. His guitar had a worn patch under his strumming hand and he smiled as he sang.

We learned many new songs that we had never heard before. Goodbye Fred Rogers. I will miss you Friendly Giant. Move over Mr. Dressup and welcome in Mr. Bob Dylan, Original Caste, and Mr. James Taylor. We sang "Blowing in the Wind," "One Tin Soldier," and "You've got a Friend" over and over again. Music was no longer trapped in that tiny kitchen radio—it was alive, I had seen someone make it and knew now that I could make it too.

What is most interesting to me about this stage in our lives is how we process music. The brain undergoes rapid neural development during the first years of life, with new neural networks being formed more rapidly than at any other time. Our brain doesn't keep what we don't feel we need, or, more accurately, we don't keep what we don't use or replay. The brain goes through many processes in helping us interpret the music we hear. Our ears become attuned to certain styles and textures that are especially intriguing to us.

Do you remember what style of music you were drawn to at this time? Perhaps you heard certain music in your home? An older sibling's room? Outside the neighbors' house? That's what I want you to explore in this age category—those styles and textures you gravitated toward in the music you remember. These can be accessed again and used as positive triggers.

Think about your grade-school music and the songs you learned then. Perhaps you had a Mr. Trudea in your life.

Tune in and write them into your personal soundtrack.

Teen Years

▶

When I was a teen, I was no athlete, but several of my friends were. Carolyn was the most talented, natural athlete in school. Her long legs and long hair were a blur as she seemed to just float above the surface of the earth, and no one, especially me, could keep up to her. That did not deter me from wanting to be her close friend. At recess, she would teach me wonderful tricks that I could do on the monkey bars, and we would practice walking across the top and doing triple axel-ish flips off the sides of the posts.

I was on my third try to get the flip just right when I landed on the ground and heard a terrible crack. I saw my ankle pointing awkwardly. My mind went blank as a teacher came and carried me into the school. Mom picked me up and took me to the doctor. The timing could not have been worse. It was Halloween and my costume was waiting at home. This would have been the first year that I was allowed to go trick-or-treating with a large group of fun friends without our parents tagging along.

The doctors were able to set a cast with mortar, but that did nothing to raise my spirits or stem the profound disappointment I was feeling. The only thing that could turn this disaster around was something better than going out with my friends on Halloween and more distracting than my broken ankle. The answer came in the form of a surprise gift.

As I lay, dejected, in my bed at home, Mom reached into a plastic bag and pulled out a thin, square cardboard package. I sat up and unwrapped her gift, speechless as I saw the face on the front of the album. Staring back at me was my childhood heartthrob — Shaun Cassidy. With his blue eyes and wavy blonde hair, I could feel Shaun looking right through me. I forgot about what I was missing that evening. It took me a full hour to carefully unwrap and play the entire album while flipping through the inner pages of quotes, photos, and song lyrics. Mission accomplished... I was completely absorbed.

∎

Whenever I have my music therapy participants begin to explore their music choices from their teen years, the triggers come fast and furious. That time of our lives seems to produce some of our most strongly anchored music memories—songs that can take us back to a period when we were often rocked by intense emotions and situations. When I think back to all the music of my teen years, I remember lying on my girlfriend's bed, listening to ABBA and the Bee Gees. I had a feeling of belonging and acceptance. Music filled me up, and whenever I hear those songs, those same warm feelings come rushing back.

As teens, we have a very personal and self-centered relationship with music. Throughout those years, music seems to be intrinsically linked to our forming of our personal identity. More than any other time in our life, we appropriate and personalize songs, validating and internalizing our moments of angst, frustration, and joy with the lyrics and melodies. As adults, we often revisit the music of our teen years when life's load gets too heavy and we need a boost or want to rediscover that carefree feeling of our youth.

If you were a teen in the '70s, chances are you forever will move to Queen, Stevie Wonder, and ABBA. If you were young in the '90s, "Wannabe" by the Spice Girls might get you back on that dance floor. At any age, music seems to be associated with positive emotional memories with social themes, bringing back the positive impressions from the events that shaped us all through our lives. This is why music can help us to improve our life satisfaction during the challenging times we all inevitably will face.

During our teen years music seems to be associated with a lot of firsts: first dance, first kiss, first love, first breakup. Perhaps that is why the music of our teen years seems to linger far into adulthood, if not forever.

The music from your teen years may need a bit more space— don't be afraid to expand this section of your personal soundtrack.

Adulthood to Today

As we enter adulthood, we leave behind many of the social pressures that can go along with listening to music. As adults, our preferences become more settled and we tend to stick with our favorite radio stations and albums. But we continue to establish new associations between music and personal encounters, so it is important to record those on your chart as well.

It may be my age, but I have certainly been experiencing a higher level of reflection in my life. Perhaps I'm even looking for opportunities to reflect? This book has certainly helped with that. As much as I continue to explore new music introduced to me by my clients or my children, I have definitely become one of "those people"— the ones who listen to "oldies music" like my mom used to do. The familiar music from my past, sometimes the very distant past, reminds me of the young person I once was. There have been many times when I have wanted to reach back in time and be able to tell my younger self, "You will be just fine."

For many of us, our personal soundtrack in our later adult years becomes more than just a memory—it can become our legacy, for others to remember us by.

▶

For Gwen, music enabled her to become all that she could be with only a month left to live. A fifty-five-year-old mother and nurse, she sat in a warmly decorated room near the window. Sixteen months prior, she had been diagnosed with cancer. Now, her world had narrowed to a hospice room near the outskirts of town. Gwen did all she could in her fragile state to prepare her loved ones for the inevitable.

When I was introduced to Gwen, she was wearing a colorful headscarf that covered what had once been a head full of shiny blond hair. Pictures of her and her family were all around the room, interspersed with bright paintings and drawings.

"Come, sit close to me. I have been expecting you," she said. "I need you to help me."

Gwen asked me to open the small desk drawer and remove the small stack of papers that rested inside. I looked at the twelve songs in front of me. "Will you please meet us here precisely at 2:00 p.m. on Friday and play these songs on your guitar?"

That Friday, I had the songs prepared and arrived right at 2:00 p.m. Gwen's daughter and sister were already there, seated on either side of her. "Thank you for coming," she said as she gestured for me to sit on a chair in the corner. She seemed to gather herself, sitting up a little higher in her bed before turning to address her daughter and her sister.

"I invited you here today because we need to say goodbye." Silence. "I know that this is hard for you as it is for me, so I came up with an idea that could perhaps help all of us. Hailey, will you please go into the side closet and take out the piece of canvas I asked Julia to bring last week?" Hailey walked over to the closet, opened the door, and brought out the canvas leaning against the wall inside. "Julia will you please reach into that top drawer and bring out the pastels that one of the nurses brought for me?" Julia walked to the end of the bed and opened the top drawer to find the pastels. There were many colors.

When the two women were once again seated on either side of Gwen, she continued to speak. "I have asked Jennifer to play twelve songs today. During the first song, I am going to start drawing, and when the song ends, I am going to pass the canvas to you, Julia, and you are going to continue the picture, adding in whatever the music brings to your mind.

"When the second song is finished, you will pass the canvas to Hailey, who is going to continue from where you left off. We will pass the canvas back and forth after every song."

Soon it was time for the last song. I was nervous as I strummed the first few chords, knowing there would be no more pastels or passing of the canvas, only time to reflect on what had been created. As the last piece, Gwen had selected "What a Wonderful World," the highly emotional song famously performed by Louis Armstrong, and on this day, the images it called to mind were perfectly reflected.

Gwen put a few finishing strokes on the canvas and then held it up for each of them to look at. They had had created a painting of a beautiful meadow with flowers of many colors. Six weeks later the image would be screened onto a CD cover and the twelve songs would be shared with every person who attended her funeral. Gwen's Signature Twelve.

I carefully put the canvas on a high shelf facing down toward them so the women could see it as it dried. Then I quietly left the room so they could continue their goodbye.

❚❚

Gwen had set the intention of using her life's musical soundtrack as the backdrop to already powerful relationships. It was a non-verbal means of sharing herself and her heart to help her loved ones heal, and the songs she had so carefully selected allowed her to say a touching goodbye.

Gwen left me the gift of one of the most powerful exercises I have experienced in my career—taking ALL the music that matters most and curating it down to only twelve pieces.

♪ **YOUR SIGNATURE 12**

Even though you may not have quite completed charting your personal soundtrack, you have probably landed on many or most of the songs, albums, and artists that were most significant to you.

If narrowing your choices down to just a dozen seems impossible, this may be all the more reason why that's exactly what you should do. Perhaps even more telling than what you *do* select may be the music you choose *not* to include in your top twelve— that will open up even deeper insights into who you are and what you value. The act of building such a specialized playlist can bring forth some new clues about what music means to you that you may not have considered yet.

Music is very personal and can do a lot of heavy lifting, emotionally. It can give us that hug when we need it the most. Remember that the closer we get to our music, the clearer our vision will become. I can't think of a better way of hastening this process than by reviewing your personal soundtrack and taking it that extra step—identify your Signature 12.

Looking Through the Wellness, Wellplayed Lens

We are always collecting music. Some of our collection gets released over time and temporarily forgotten while other music memories endure throughout our lifetime. However, under the right circumstances, all music is retrievable—meaning that we can remember it when the conditions are right. What you may find most interesting about the personal soundtrack exercise, though, is the realization that, by taking time to look at our music history, we can step back from our lives and see ourselves in a more objective way—which can feel very therapeutic.

Our earliest music memories are some of the most enduring memories we may have. Pay particular attention to these and to the feelings that are evoked when you think of them. I remember the first time Mr Trudea sang "One Tin Soldier." To this day, I recall every word as if I had just learned it yesterday. Remembering him turning toward us kids and teaching us a "grown-up" song conjures feelings of belonging.

Our lives can be documented with music. Everyone has a unique personal soundtrack that highlights the bumps, joys, and bruises of life. Movies, television, live experiences, passive listening—all contribute to our personal soundtrack. The fact that we don't tend to add much music to our soundtracks beyond the age of thirty is interesting. Perhaps that is why we all end up listening to the oldies station at some point in our lives. I have also noticed, however (and my children are an example), that many children like to listen to the same music we once did. I mean *exactly* the same. The same artist. The same song. My personal soundtrack is now meshed with those of my friends, my family, and my children. Because of their music preferences, I have broadened my personal soundtrack.

As we begin to order and curate our personal soundtrack, we rediscover old things and learn new things about ourselves. If we were to look at our list through the eyes of a music therapist, we would see, not just music, but also times where there are gaps or sudden shifts in your preferences. These gaps, or periods of musical silence, most likely also mean something.

It may have been that you were distracted by something else at the time—perhaps a new love, a new sport? A big move? Or it could have been something else, like a disappointing divorce, or the loss of someone dear. Take a moment and honor these music-free interludes. They had their own beat. If you feel they might signify something you may not have completely processed, finding someone to work through it with, a professional or otherwise, can really help.

As we begin to share our life's soundtrack with others we will also begin to hear differences in our song stories. Some may not resemble the one we have curated due to being of different age or growing up on a different continent. By remaining curious, interested, and asking questions along the way, our active listening to another's soundtrack will reveal new childhood experiences, cultural context, and associated memories. Certainly a growth opportunity for all.

When words are not enough, let music start the conversation.

TRACK
5

Playlists to Activate Your Memory

"Music is life itself."

LOUIS ARMSTRONG

ALMOST TWENTY YEARS ago, researchers at Dartmouth College successfully identified the area of the brain where music memories are stored.

The study was published in the March 9, 2005 issue of *Nature* and titled "Sound of Silence Activates Auditory Cortex." In it, the Dartmouth team found that, even if a song was missing short snippets, study participants could mentally fill in the blanks as they listened, provided the song was familiar to them. "We played music in the scanner [fMRI], and then we hit a virtual 'mute' button," said one author of the study. "We found that people couldn't help continuing the song in their heads, and when they did this, the auditory cortex remained active even though the music had stopped."

"It's fascinating that although the ear isn't actually hearing the song, the brain is perceptually hearing it," said another author.

Strong emotions help to embed experiences in the brain and turn them into long-lasting memories. We associate songs with feelings, people, and places. I've always found it interesting that, when someone requests a song, whether during a music therapy session or at the piano bar, they will always choose one that evokes positive memories. I can't think of the last time (or any time really) when I've heard someone pick a song they believed would evoke negative feelings. Although there is plenty of rhetoric that suggests we are wired more for negative news and images, my experience suggests the opposite is true with music.

"Music often accompanies emotional events," says one music psychologist. She goes on to suggest that the reason we recall events and emotions so vividly in our memories may be because the music itself is highly evocative and emotional. For Harry this was certainly the case.

▶

Harry

It was just before Christmas when Harry invited me to spend an evening with him and his family. The suggestion I should come to his home to facilitate a music-filled evening included a very compelling reason: "It is the first time in ten years that all my children will be home for Christmas, and I want to make it special for them."

He went on to explain, "You said that by giving people a choice of song, you are giving every person a voice and an opportunity to teach you something about themselves. I want to hear what is important to my children and create an evening to remember." How could I resist?

It certainly was an evening to remember—full of songs, stories, emotions, and heartfelt family spirit. Music, the consummate connector, was at work again, keeping Harry's family entertained and, more importantly, helping them to tap into their feelings about the people around them and the experiences they were sharing. The songs were recorded and became part of a Family Christmas Playlist for everyone to take home as their gift from Harry.

A month later, I received the following letter.

Dear Jennifer,

I can't thank you enough for coming to my home at Christmas time. It was the "special time" I knew it would be. What I didn't mention to you then is that I have been experiencing extreme and unusual mood swings. These changes in behavior have been very difficult and frustrating for

*my family. They have been very worried. Just shortly after Christmas
I was given the diagnosis I was expecting. I have Alzheimer's disease.
Last Christmas may be my last Christmas I remember with my family.
I hope the music will continue to trigger the special memories we shared
that evening.*

Thank you for the gift of music.

Harry

❚❚

As strongly as music can be used to help us remember, perhaps it
is equally as good at helping us forget the other things going on in
our life just for a while. It doesn't get rid of the cause of our stresses,
but it can create space around our spirit, for a few hours or even for
a few minutes, and give us relief from those stresses. We can use
that space to help find a glimpse of where we want to go and maybe
even give us the resolve to find a way to get there.

Start a Music Hub

The enjoyment people derive from getting together after reading
a great book to share personal connections and insights has made
book clubs very popular. You can find them online, in coffee shops,
and through bookstores. Which begs the question: How about a
music club? A music hub? A place where music lovers are looking
to meet fellow music lovers. A place to show off our tastes and learn
what others like. A great way to encourage us to pay attention to our
current listening habits while also discovering new music. A place
to dig deeply into our memories and to create new ones. Perhaps
you can already envision the perfect group of old or new friends you
feel would be interested in getting together to talk music?

♪ **HOSTING A MUSIC HUB**

If you find the concept as intriguing as I do, here are six steps to get you started.

1. Determine What Type of Music Hub You Want to Host.
Just like a book club, your music hub can be highly social, seriously academic, or a combination of both. Maybe you want to start a music hub that focuses on your country's homegrown music, or perhaps it will travel around the globe. Or perhaps you'll want to keep the emphasis on getting to know the people in the club, as well as their music preferences. Setting a theme can help you make all the other decisions about how your music hub will look, so, whatever your focus (or lack thereof!), *make sure you determine what it is* (or determine as a group at your first meet-up) so everyone can buy into the same mission.

2. Figure Out Who You Will Welcome to Join.
Whether your music hub will be hosted just for you and a friend or will bring together a large group of strangers you've met online, it's important to have a handle on who will be able to join. Will you invite close friends only? Do you want to expand your social circle and welcome anyone who's interested? Big groups can offer a wider variety of ideas and viewpoints, but smaller gatherings can be more intimate and allow you the opportunity to really build relationships. Keep in mind that the size of your music hub will also dictate when and where you can meet, and whether it will be in-person or virtual.

3. Decide Where Your Music Hub Will Meet.
Once you know *who* you're inviting, or at least have an idea of how many people to expect, the next thing to consider is *how* you'll meet. A music hub doesn't necessarily have to meet physically. Online platforms make it easy to share music through computers.

If you prefer to host a music hub that meets physically, consider how much space you'll need. Whether in-person or online, sound quality is always a significant consideration. That's why music hubs, unlike book clubs, are not the best candidates for the coffee-shop environment. Private homes and offices are the most suitable venues for in-person gatherings, and for virtual meetings, a training session for members to optimize their online environments will need to be one of the first items on the agenda.

Some music hubs run both virtually and physically, either alternating online and in-person discussions or running both at the same time. Setting up a private social media page may be useful in this case, so participants can review the listening recommendations from that week or month at their leisure. Think about what will work best for your group of music lovers.

4. Think About How Best to Access the Music.
Each member will need to consider how they will access their new music. Will they purchase entire albums, buy individual songs, or subscribe to streaming services? Depending on individual circumstances, including means and opportunity, members may want to consider purchasing the music they are using and learning about, as a way to support the contributing artists.

5. Facilitate Great Discussion.
You've figured out all the details, everyone is happy with the concept you've chosen for your music hub, and you're excited to host your first session. Now...what are you going to talk about? Always have an opening question. There have been several scattered throughout this book that could serve as inspiration. (I would be really jazzed to learn that this book served as the focus for your hybrid book/music hub!)

Even if you've listened to a song over and over throughout your entire life, guiding a music hub discussion (or any discussion for that matter) can be a little daunting, so framing it around the day's theme or question can be useful. As you move into future meetings, it will be increasingly important for members to know the themes and questions in advance, as it will take some preparation on their part to be ready to participate fully. Listening to inspiring music and engaging in discussions about music and life as a group is a great way to promote positive interaction and make people feel good.

6. Be Mindful of the Logistics.
It can be easy to overlook some of the little details, but they can make or break the experience. Consider and decide:

- How often will your music hub meet?
- How will members share music?
- What time is best to meet that supports a variety of schedules?
- How will communications be dispatched? (e.g., private social media group or email list)
- How will homework for the next meeting be assigned?

Looking Through the Wellness, Wellplayed Lens

Music's incredible capacity to trigger memories is one of the core tenets of music therapy, driving much of the music therapist's treatment design. Used with the right intention, frequency, and intensity, music has the power to transform feelings of being totally lost into feelings of being comforted and less alone.

Most of the time, music conjures up positive memories—but sometimes it doesn't. A few years back, I did several interviews on the national news, sharing my perspective on a study by clinical psychologist Linda Blair concerning the potentially negative effects of Christmas music (too early, too repetitive, not good for everyone's emotional state, etc.).

I put it this way: Christmas music is everywhere and, at least for some people, it seems to be starting earlier and earlier each year. The first bars of "Rocking Around the Christmas Tree" can bring memories of Christmas Past flooding back and, for some, a happiness chord is struck, joy is released, a lightness that was missing settles in for the month. Yet for many others, Christmas music brings on different, much less enjoyable feelings. Such people may hear Christmas music and feel immediately agitated and annoyed. They quickly reach for the wine bottle and crank up their favorite rock album. More seriously for others, the sound of Christmas music triggers worse feelings than tension, replacing carefree thoughts with the deep ache of grief and loss.

But rest assured—there are steps we can take to help us make it through the difficult seasons we will all inevitably face.

♪ MAKING MUSIC WORK FOR YOU DURING DIFFICULT TIMES

1. Use Silence as Required.
I understand that there are times we cannot remove ourselves from the music—at a friend's house, walking through the mall—but we can still find many opportunities to take a moment, step away, and find the necessary stillness we seek. Music is a blend of sound and silence. If life is music and music is life, then silence is a necessary part of both.

2. Introduce New Music Into Your Personal Soundtrack.
With today's technology and the ease with which we can listen

to music on demand, it's a great time to introduce yourself to brand-new music, to massage your auditory cortex and your imagination. Music stimulates creativity by increasing blood and oxygen flow to the brain, taking us from sleepy brain to stimulated brain. We often feel our happiest when we embrace our creativity, and music can help us get there.

3. Listen to Seasonal Music With No Lyrics— and Perhaps a New Rhythm.

If you identify yourself as a Non-Preferred-Christmas-Listener (NPCL), but your mom is coming over to bake her best shortbread, may I suggest sampling Christmas music with no lyrics and a new beat (think "Christmas reggae")? During cookie-baking season this can be particularly helpful!

4. Listen to Music That Soothes.

The right music relaxes the mind and lowers cortisol levels, helping you breathe throughout a high-stress season. When used intentionally, there is ample evidence to suggest music can make a difference in lowering anxiety and reducing your stress. Some research suggests that listening to music that soothes is as effective as taking 10 mg of valium. That's powerful stuff.

5. Use Music to Feel Connected to Those Who Have Passed.

Music is a powerful anchor that roots people to one another. If a friend or family member has passed away, hearing "their music" can make the missing that much more profound. If silence (#1) is not available to you it may be time to take a few minutes to lean into the feelings of loss. A single song may still connect you, and although tears may flow, perhaps that feeling of connection is what you needed. When the grief becomes too difficult to bear, please reach out to a friend, family member, or professional. It is not healthy to go through grief alone, and you don't have to.

6. Socialize to Your Favorite Music.
Go out and hear live music! Take along a few people you enjoy spending time with. Nothing is stopping you from creating new, more positive memories for future years to come.

By now, you have identified much of your music from your personal history as well as your current listening habits. You likely have begun to hear music in a new way, not just as something you passively experience, but as something you can actively choose to control. While these exercises may seem simple, they can have a profound effect.

TRACK
6

Playlists to Regulate Your Mood

"A great song should lift your heart, warm the soul and make you feel good."

COLBIE CAILLAT

MUSIC IS OFTEN referred to as a universal language, but it is really more of a universal art form with the capacity to evoke powerful emotions that transcend cultural and linguistic boundaries. Listening to a favorite song triggers a common pattern of brain activity, regardless of genre. That may explain why different people describe similar emotions and memory responses when listening to their favorite piece of music, whether it's a recording of Bach, Joni Mitchell, or Tupac.

Your preferences are your greatest triggers to snap you into the mood you want to be in. Marketing research has really taken this to heart. Companies spend huge amounts of time and money learning what kind of music (or no music at all) will most effectively draw customers to their retail outlets and advertisements.

I once had a woman say to me, "I hate when I walk into a store that is playing music I don't like," to which I replied, "Perhaps you are not the demographic they are marketing to." She said she had never thought about that before.

There is a long-held theory that suggests there is a part of our mind that can recognize patterns within complex data, but that we are hardwired to find simple patterns more pleasurable. This does not imply that human beings are simple, but it does seem to suggest that the mind likes to make sense of what it hears. So, whether you are a die-hard classicist or a pop diva, it seems you choose the music you prefer according to how you feel when you hear it.

Music can help us change a negative or resistant emotional state into a positive, learning state. But it can also do the exact opposite— the wrong music (tone, style) can distract us or even send us into a deep funk for some time afterward. Connecting to the music in our playlists is the first step toward having it help change our emotional state. The next step is learning how to intentionally use our playlists to affect our emotions—proactively bending the power of music to do our bidding, whether we need an emotional boost or support and comfort during difficult times.

What music would help you feel better immediately, motivate you, and charge you up so you don't feel so overwhelmed? The piece you choose should take you out of your current emotional state and move you into your more desired and needed state.

Researchers have pondered the potential therapeutic and mood-boosting benefits of music for centuries. For many listeners, even sad music can bring pleasure as it works to validate and console, according to recent research from Durham University in the United Kingdom and the University of Jyväskylä in Finland. The authors of the study suggest that sad music can provide a substitute for a lost relationship—perhaps another reason why so many of us gravitate to it during times of grief and loss. Music can become that empathic friend, an ally who truly understands you and what you are going through. But this study also brings up the rationale for engaging a music therapist to process our feelings. Professor Jörg Fachner, who reviewed the study, suggests, "a skillful, trained music therapist can sense and adapt to the individual meaning of the sad music representing negative experiences and memories."

There are also reams of research on the joy that music can bring. A 2013 study in *The Journal of Positive Psychology* found that people who listened to music they found to be upbeat could improve their moods and boost their happiness in just two weeks. In a press release, lead author Yuna Ferguson noted that happiness has been linked to better physical health, higher income, and greater relationship satisfaction.

♪ RHYTHM OF LIFE

This exercise starts with a very simple graph.

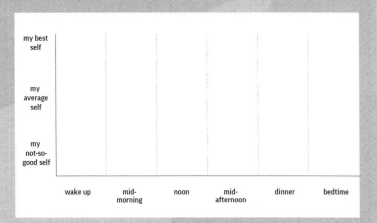

Along the Y axis (left side), you have three mood states. I have purposefully kept these vague, because we are all going to have completely unique ways of describing our "best" self versus our "average" or "not-so-good" self. However, it is really important for you to define these states in as much detail as possible to ensure this activity is intentional and you derive the greatest benefit from it.

I am going to use myself as an example:

My best self: productive, smiling, wanting to connect to other humans, everything seems easier because I am happy.

My average self: relaxed, focused, able to work through a whole day but tired by the end.

My not-so-good self: overwhelmed or tired to the bone, not wanting to see even one more person, craving only wine and dessert for dinner.

The next step is to plot positions on the graph to show whatever "self" you typically feel like as you move throughout your day: when you wake up, at mid-morning, noon, mid-afternoon, and around dinnertime.

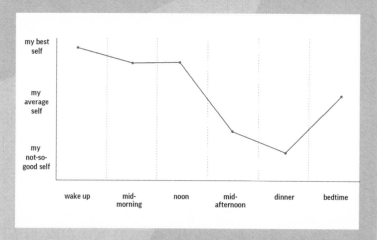

In other words, when you wake up, are you usually feeling like your best self, like me? OR do you tend to need some time before you begin to wake up and feel somewhat inspired or motivated?

Keep in mind there is NO right, wrong, or judgment implied here—the world is full of morning people, afternoon people, and night people. I just happen to be one of the morning people (because it is the best time of day, of course!). A lot of people who feel their best self in the morning feel completely different in the evening. And there are other people who will say they are steadily their average self throughout the course of an entire day, and still others who are at their best in the evening.

After you've filled in the dots describing how you feel throughout these different times of day, draw a line to connect them, so you can actually see how your energy fluctuates throughout a typical day. Does it go up (and when?) or does it go down (and why?). The line may be pretty much level, or it may go up or down a lot, just like your own personal rhythm—your heartbeat.

The purpose of this exercise is to draw your attention to the rhythms of your average day. How do you feel about it? Is there some time of day that you feel you may want to try to change?

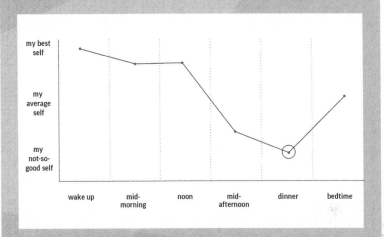

Circle one time where you would like to bring about a 10-percent change (up or down). For example, if you are a morning person, you may want to strive for a 10-percent upward shift around dinnertime. Or, if your energy feels too high at night, you may want to bring it down a bit sooner in the evening so you can have a more restful sleep.

To see any shift in your life, you first need to have a shift in your feelings.

As you consider that one time of day when you would most like to see a 10-percent shift, ask yourself what it might take to make that shift happen. What feeling do you need to introduce?

Looking at my chart, you may feel that I need energy, and that would be a really good guess. But I have to tell you, when I hit that dinner hour after being active since 5:00 or 5:30 in the morning, the very thought of feeling energetic just depletes me more. What I feel I need most at that time of day is some quiet, a moment to feel nurtured, and the chance to refuel—not just with food, but with feelings of safety and comfort.

Ask yourself: What feeling would help you experience a 10-percent shift at the time of day you seem to need it most? Try to keep it to one word. Here are some examples:

Enthusiasm	Solitude	Energy
Focus	Stillness	Creativity
Inspiration	Safety	Joy
Freedom	Connection	Comfort

So now you have your word. One word. One feeling that you want to add to one time of day so you feel 10 percent better.

That one word *is* the name of your playlist. Not "Favorite R&B," not "Soothing Soul"—but the exact feeling you want to achieve at that time of day. Say, "Stillness," or "Freedom."

Your final task to complete this exercise is to begin filling this playlist with music selections that, every time you hear them, move you closer to your desired "one-word" feeling. If you chose "Stillness," it might be an ambient track and a jazz melody that have always made you feel calm and centered. You do not need a lot of pieces of music in this playlist; eight to twelve songs should do it, because you won't need to be listening to it for long—just for fifteen to thirty minutes, right around the time of day you need it, or shortly before.

And—you guessed it—you can do this same exercise for ANY time of day. Perhaps you need a mid-morning playlist for "Inspiration," and an evening playlist for "Serenity."

I suggest you continue to use your "Rhythm of Life" playlists for as long as they work. Don't be surprised if there comes a time when a song on one of your lists no longer evokes the feeling you aspire to. The good news is that, when that day comes, you can simply delete that song and add in a new one!

How About If We Feel Blue?

So, what kind of music do you listen to when everything seems to be a bit bluer than usual? Lots? Some? None? Finding the right combination of music mixed with silence can be one way to validate and recover from temporary sadness. That is, unless you have stopped listening to music entirely, as I did eighteen years ago.

After safely delivering my beautiful daughter, I quietly slipped into a deep melancholic state—without even realizing it. The result? I completely stopped listening to music for pleasure. Fourteen months after my daughter was born, I remember being stopped at a red light and having the sudden desire to tune in to a station I had once loved to listen to. The moment I turned that dial, I learned two things about myself: 1) that I had been depressed without knowing it, and 2) today was the day I finally felt a bit better. I remember smiling to myself as I continued through the green light—and on with the rest of my life. An old song I've always loved was playing and I felt lighter than I had for months.

My NOT listening to music was a clear indicator that my mood had altered, stealthily progressing into what I now know was undiagnosed postpartum depression. Over the years, I have worked with countless individuals who had drastically changed their musical listening interests or stopped listening to music altogether, depending on what point they were at in their cycle of sadness.

Here is some good news: Research shows that listening to music can definitely lift your mood and help you feel strengthened, so if you are having a blue day, you may want to reach for music—and not necessarily happy music, but music that reflects and supports your current emotional state.

Anchor Songs

In my first book, *Tune In*, I talk about the way music triggers us and anchors us to an emotional state. Anchor songs can fix us firmly to a certain feeling, and, as we discussed earlier, the right feeling at the right time lures us into action. Some very skilled persuaders, including political leaders, have found theme songs to be their greatest ally in influencing large groups of people.

Think about the last political rally you watched on TV. Did you notice the choice of song? Did you feel it was a good fit? Did it highlight their message, or perhaps even their values? Of course, music has not necessarily always been in the interests of the greater good; however, as a vehicle for helping people feel connected and inspiring a shared state of courageous camaraderie, the use of such songs is often highly effective.

Television programs use anchor songs all the time, as a way to hold the attention of viewers and set the desired emotional state for the scene. Oftentimes, the same piece of music will be played again later in the program to serve as a reminder, or to let us know that an issue has been resolved. I remember a popular show of its day, *Ally McBeal*, where music was used as a primary character in the series, highlighting the lead actors' emotions. The music anchored the viewer to the recurring feelings of McBeal (played by Calista Flockhart). For example, a memorable hallucination of a dancing "baby" would show up accompanied by the tune "Hooked on a Feeling" by B.J. Thomas. This music anchor would represent one of McBeal's biggest fears: missing the biological window to have a baby of her own.

Music is a powerful persuader with the potential to take your emotions just about anywhere. More examples of this are all over TV shows—especially police shows and hospital or doctor dramas. Music plays in the background as the actors go about the most mundane activities—driving down the street, looking through binoculars, identifying the drug used at a crime scene. Most important of all is the music background for the lab analysis scene. They do it all with music building in the background to help manufacture a sense of action or suspense, or to convey vulnerable moments.

While there are many commercial entities that have their own theme songs, I'm a huge proponent of personal anchor songs. These are songs that trigger memories very quickly and act as our personal anthems. An anchor song prepares our psyche for whatever the world chooses to throw at us, and makes an important moment that much more meaningful.

An anchor song becomes so ingrained in our psyche that it anchors us to an emotional state the instant we hear it. There are a number of ways you can incorporate these theme songs into your daily life.

♩ **CREATE YOUR ANCHOR**

Here are a few ideas to get you started. Choose songs with the specific intent to trigger the following feelings:

- "first thing in the morning" songs to anchor the tone of your home and give you a sense of stability.

- "get ready for school" songs that motivate you for the day ahead.

- "mealtime with the family" songs that promote socializing and a sense of comfort.

- "study so I get an A" songs that helps you feel focused.

- "relax after a stressful day" songs that take you from feeling chaotic to calm in minutes.

- "celebrating special holiday" songs that spark a sense of joy and togetherness

- any songs that inspire any other feeling you'd like to experience in the next fifteen minutes.

Looking Through the Wellness, Wellplayed Lens

Let's talk about entrainment as we take another look at the music therapist's perspective through the Wellness, Wellplayed lens. Our mood often seems to correlate directly with our sense of connection—both with others and with ourselves. The word "entrainment" describes the "merging with, or synchronizing to, the pulse of the music." This principle is related to the isomorphic principle, which states that one's mood can match the mood of the music and then gradually move with the music.

The principle of entrainment is universal and has applications in chemistry, pharmacology, biology, medicine, psychology, sociology, astronomy, architecture, and more. The classic example shows individual pulsing heart muscle cells which, as they are brought closer together, begin pulsing in synchronicity. Another example of the entrainment effect is when two or more women living in the same household find after a time that their menstrual cycles have synchronized.

The entrainment process is everywhere in music. It is possible to have rhythmic entrainment, melodic entrainment, and dynamic entrainment. Entrainment music has the potential to resonate with the listener's feelings, transform negativity into positivity, and promote a state of liveliness or serenity.

Entrainment also describes the tendency of two oscillating bodies to lock into phase, so that they vibrate in harmony. This leads me to believe that, when people say they are lonely or looking for ways to connect, what they mean is that they are looking for someone who understands and "gets it"—perhaps what they are really seeking is someone to entrain with.

TRACK
7

Playlists to Boost Your Motivation

"If people take anything from my music, it should be motivation to know that anything is possible as long as you keep working at it and don't back down."

EMINEM

MUSIC IS AN invitation to action. It invites you into the main auditorium when you're attending a conference, it generates anticipation as the theme song plays at the start of your favorite TV show, it cues your mind and body to prepare you for the next movement at the gym.

In her book *The Power of Music,* Elena Mannes highlights how music affects different people and their actions. For example, infants seem to prefer smooth versus dissonant, jarring sounds. This probably isn't surprising as many of us recognize the natural instinct to move back and forth evenly and gently while humming and holding a wee one. Rocking babies to sleep, to quiet your cries— and those of the infant too—is one of our most natural movements, dating back to our earliest ancestors. Add in some cooing and, well, you must be participating in one of the oldest movement and music combinations in history.

And then there is dancing. In Track 2 we learned how music is like a dance in the brain, moving all over. Well, there is more that stimulates our brains' reward centers, including coordinated movements. Consider the thrill some people get from clapping as others dance at a party or watching a choreographed fight scene in an action movie. The synchronizing of music and movement truly doubles our reward.

But it is not just rocking or dancing that can feel so good. In 1959, a doctor named H.R. Teirich undertook one of the earliest studies into the therapeutic effects of music and vibration. He built a couch containing loudspeakers that transferred the vibrations from J.S. Bach's *Toccata and Fugue in D minor* straight to the solar plexus. He enlisted his fellow doctors as a subject group. They reported immediate warmth in the solar plexus, a feeling of complete relaxation, and then a big burst of optimism—exactly what the doctors needed to get back to work.

So how does rocking, dancing, and feeling vibration in the lower abdomen relate to motivation? Why are we talking about movement when this track is called Playlists to Boost Your Motivation? Well, it seems that movement and motivation are closely aligned—and the ultimate spark to getting you feeling motivated and into action is the right music at the right time.

A friend of mine loves to put on the latest hip-hop whenever she's doing tough physical work around the house, like cleaning out the garage or carrying items up from the basement. For her, music creates a blend of feelings—relaxed, productive, and motivated all at the same time. This feelings combination seems to make the heavier tasks lighter.

All actions seem to require momentum and endurance. That sounds like motivation to me. And interestingly, music appears to draw out seemingly opposite feelings simultaneously to provide all the support it can. A coupling of optimism with relaxation, enthusiasm with less stress, inspiration with a sense of peace.

Have you ever experienced a similar phenomenon? Two different feelings that give you a boost of optimism and motivation?

The rest of this track is going to look at three particular contexts:

1 How does music personally motivate you day to day?
2 How does music motivate you at (or for) work?
3 And how does music influence your movement and sports performance?

Let's start by inviting music to open our mind and heart and giving ourselves permission to try something new.

Mindset and Music

American psychologist Carol Dweck has famously introduced many to the belief that mindset matters, and that you can either be in a growth state of mind or a fixed state of mind. If a growth mindset sounds appealing, there is much evidence that seeking out new music, giving it a chance and learning more about it, can flex your auditory muscle and help you achieve that positive state of mind that helps you grow.

One of the biggest joys you will likely derive from making and sharing playlists will come from giving people the gift of new music. New music, new growth.

Of course, "new" doesn't have to mean *literally* new. It could refer to digging up an old gem or re-contextualizing seemingly unrelated songs. Either way, a great playlist should include an element of surprise or wonder or discovery that elevates it beyond a collection of solid tunes to provide that boost of optimism we all need.

You may have seen one of the new streaming channels dedicated to young people experiencing old music for the first time—sharing their commentary as they listen, describing their aesthetic response to the song and the feelings it inspires. As we watch and listen to their first encounter with "new music," we can benefit by experiencing the music as if for the first time too—but with a fresh perspective through the eyes (and ears) of someone else. Watching their youthful expressions, listening to them "ooh" and "ah" as their heads begin to bob and the smile shines out from their faces, you can't help but notice the influx of energy that animates their eyes and bodies as they listen.

Finding new music can help you discover new things about yourself. Going to a concert or hearing a new album (or even just one new song) can resonate so strongly that you feel the immediate need to incorporate it into your life soundtrack. I remember Mom introducing me to many female icons, including Mahalia Jackson, Lena Horne, Patti LaBelle, Annie Lennox, Melissa Etheridge, K.D. Lang, and many others. These powerhouse singers have carried through to my current-day preferences and encourage me to seek out a "type" of singer regardless of genre. Even now, their incomparable voices continue to motivate me to stand tall, speak strong, and get ready for whatever the day brings.

What Music Naturally Motivates You?

To find music that motivates you, let's start with your unique style and what you gravitate to most naturally. When I was feeling uncertain about what to wear for an upcoming conference keynote and photoshoot, I worked with personal branding expert Leela Jacobs. Before looking through my wardrobe or taking me shopping, she took the time to get to know me and, as she put it, "dig into my authentic self." She did this by asking me about my favorite hobbies, what television series engaged me the most, and what music I loved to listen to. I highly recommend you try this too.

♪ **WHAT'S YOUR JAM?**

The list is long and growing, but what genres motivate you the most? If you don't recognize a style, this is a great opportunity to do a search and grow with new music. It is also an opportunity to learn about what styles of music motivate others, helping us to develop that growth mindset and a world view full of curiosity and interest.

Which of these genres motivate you the most?

- A capella
- Afrobeats
- Bachata
- Baila
- Balada
- Benga
- Bossa nova
- Bollywood
- Carnatic
- Celtic chant
- Chinese folk
- Chinese traditional opera
- Chimurenga
- C-pop
- Calypso
- Compas
- Country
- Cumbia
- Dancehall
- Dangdut
- Drum & bass
- Euro-disco
- Electronic dance music (EDM)

- Ethio-jazz
- Flamenco
- Gagaku court music
- Glitch pop
- Gnawa/eth-no-pop/gwani blues
- Goa trance
- Grime
- Highlife
- Hindustani
- Hip-hop
- Hiplife
- Indie rock
- Inkiranya
- Japanese folk
- Jazz
- J-pop
- Juju
- K-pop
- K-trot
- Majika
- Mambo
- Mariachi
- Mbalax
- Mento
- Merengue

- Metal
- Ndombolo
- Oldies
- Palm wine
- Pop
- Punjabi
- Punk
- Rababah
- Rafi
- Raga rock
- Rap
- Reggae
- Rhythm & blues (R&B)
- Rock
- Rocksteady
- Opera
- Polka
- Salsa
- Ska
- Soca
- Steel band music/pan music
- Techno
- Trance
- V-pop
- Zouk

What we gravitate to means something. And it turns out that the music we listen to is no different. In a study of 36,000 participants from around the world, researchers studied the connection between musical tastes and personality types. They concluded that there does seem to be some relationship between your personality and the music that you like to listen to. The 36,000 people were asked to rate 104 musical styles, each of which were assigned certain qualities. To complete the study, the participants were also asked to answer questions about their own personalities.

Here are the most prevalent personality traits that were identified as being associated with the most popular musical preferences:

Pop	Extroverted, honest, conventional, hardworking, high self-esteem. Less creative and more uneasy.
Rap and Hip-Hop	High self-esteem and outgoing.
Country	Hardworking, conventional, outgoing, emotionally stable, more conservative. Lower ranking on the trait of openness to experience.
Rock/Heavy Metal	Quite gentle, creative, introverted. May exhibit low self-esteem.
Indie	Introverted, intellectual, and creative, but less hardworking and less gentle. Passivity, anxiousness, and low self-esteem were also identified.
Dance	Outgoing and assertive, ranks highly on the trait of openness to experience. People who preferred fast-paced electronic music also tended to rank low on gentleness.
Classical	Introverted but also at ease with themselves and the world around them. Creative with a good sense of self-esteem.
Jazz, Blues, and Soul	Extroverted with high self-esteem. Creative, intelligent, and at ease.

Of course, this is not a complete list, nor do you ever want to box yourself into one style. But the long list of genres and a large study like this can help you begin to explore new music, and start the conversation about what music gives you the energy you need when you need it most.

♪ **THE MANY SIDES OF ME—PLAY TO YOUR PERSONA**

Here is a great exercise to get to know yourself (and your work colleagues, music hub members, or any other group).

We live in a busy and stressful world, and most of us have to wear many different hats. For example, you may be a mother, daughter, sister, nana, neighbor, friend, colleague, roommate, spouse, etc., and in each one of these roles, you act and feel slightly differently. Why not create a playlist for each role? Think about what music goes best with each of the roles you fill, and put together different playlists that reflect and represent these different aspects of your identity.

Take me, for example. The four different hats I typically wear throughout the day include:

1. Jenny
Only my granny called me Jenny, and my Jenny Playlist feels like cinnamon toast on my granny's back porch with a cup of real hot cocoa, overlooking her gorgeous garden. Often it would be getting late, and would feel way past my bedtime, but that was okay—because I was at granny's house! My Jenny Playlist is not about the music I was listening to back then; it's more about the music that helps me feel the way I did when I was with her: 100-percent loved, 100-percent cared for and nurtured, all the things that made me feel so good at that time of my life. When I listen to that playlist, I feel loved.

2. JB

This is the hat I wear most of the time. This is where I am at my most productive, when I'm working an awful lot. I have my JB Playlist on and I can get a lot accomplished. It's not *always* on, though. I seem to alternate between my JB playlist and silence. And I feel it's actually that alternating rhythm—playlist, silence, playlist, silence—that helps me move through the course of my day.

3. Jennifer Buchanan

Jennifer Buchanan is a bigger, bolder persona than where I sit most of the time. She shows up whenever I have to go up on the big stage and share a really important message, that I hope matters to the audience. It's that bigger-than-life place we all need to go sometimes. For some of us, that place could be even just a social setting, or perhaps it's when we need to lead a meeting at the office without any time to prepare. My Jennifer Buchanan Playlist is the one that's playing in the car as I'm driving to a gig, setting my mind and my intention and my energy in the place where I want them to be before I enter that larger space, where I have to be a bit bigger than my normal self.

4. Stella

I envision Stella back during a bygone era, listening to Miles Davis in a dark, underground jazz and blues bar somewhere in the heart of New York City. The waiter serves a scotch, neat, to my table and I breathe in the smell of a cigar from the table in front of me. I am not there to socialize, and I am not feeling alone. I have worn my favorite red heels. The house band knows all the great standards and I can hear Ella Fitzgerald singing the selections in my mind. The persona of Stella doesn't get a chance to make an appearance very often in real life so it's nice to be able to have a playlist that reminds me so vividly of a real piece of myself, filled with jazz and blues music—my Stella Playlist.

Make Music Work at Work

Do you sometimes (or often) feel you need a boost at work? The music industry has proof that you should listen to music while you work. In a study commissioned by the UK licensing organizations PPL and PRS for Music, 77 percent of businesses surveyed found that playing music in the workplace increased staff morale and improved the atmosphere, resulting in greater productivity.

Remember—the reasons for playing music at work are numerous, and different for everyone. Keep in mind that not everyone feels more productive, creative, or inspired when listening to music. Some workers may instead feel distracted, stalled, or annoyed. This is why it is so important for all team members to participate in an honest discussion, ideally led by a keen facilitator and covering:

Benefits. Research and discuss the benefits of playing music in your work environment. For the employer, it may be boosting employee efficiency, expediting projects, and a climate of greater enthusiasm. For the staff member, it may mean sparking creativity or help in working through a project barrier.

Preferences. Organize a forum where everyone can discuss their list of preferences. This will help the release of oxytocin (the "connection" and social-bonding hormone), provided you're listening to music you like.

Playlists. Create a compilation of music that everyone is open to; this may take several days or weeks. Don't rush. Try to focus on and enjoy the process as much as the results. Developing a productive playlist for two or more people can be challenging. Like all good work procedures and strategies, it takes time, and starts with being proactive instead of reactive. Identifying the diverse needs and preferences of the group you belong to will be a slow but rewarding process.

Set guidelines. To avoid possible misunderstandings, set guidelines around when music will be played and for how long. Make sure everyone has had a chance to contribute to the playlists your group will be listening to.

Connect. One of the benefits of music at work is the way it can help you connect to your teammates. You may decide to allow individual team members to select the music on a rotating basis, so for one whole day, the team listens only to songs chosen by that one person. This can help to deepen relationships and foster a sense of connection among coworkers.

In a culturally diverse team, music can improve cross-cultural connections because it fosters cohesion and strengthens social bonds. According to music psychologist Stefan Koelsch, music connects us by affecting areas of the brain involved in empathy, trust, and cooperation. According to another study, music increases contact, coordination, and cooperation because, when we make an effort to sync with others, we tend to feel more connected and uplifted toward them.

So, although music can't solve all work-related problems, it definitely helps people feel more connected, both to themselves and to others.

Making music work at work is not always a smooth process. This is possibly the most challenging environment for finding musical common ground—which is one of the reasons why, in most work environments, people listening to music are usually doing so through their earphones or headphones. They're not sharing their music because of all the challenges we've just been discussing, and the fact that our musical tastes are so incredibly personal and preferential.

You might be interested to know that, in one study from the University of Illinois, researchers found that listening to music in all types of work settings increased work output by 6.3 percent. According to Dr. Teresa Lesiuk, people who listen to music complete their tasks more quickly and come up with better ideas than those who don't. "When you're stressed," she says, "you might make a decision more hastily; you have a very narrow focus of attention. When you're in a positive mood, you're able to take in more options."

So what does that tell us? That there's no real answer or right way to make music work at work. It depends. It's going to vary according to your work environment and the people you're working with.

But I do have one suggestion for you, particularly if you work in a setting where people seem receptive to getting to know their team members a little better. A great activity is to have one team member bring in their favorite music, and to play only that music during lunch hour. This could be a daily thing, or perhaps just every Friday. The point is, instead of looking at music as a performance enhancer for work in general, we can also use it during downtime as a way to connect with and get to know other members of our team.

Pump Up Your Workouts

I am going to start this segment with a confession—sport has never been as big a part of my life as it has been for many of my friends or family. My primary exercise has been "running" a company and "lifting up" a family. I absolutely love the outdoors and bathe frequently in our forests and lakes, but organized sport has eluded me for much of my life. I struggle to throw, run, and jump, but gosh I love to watch and cheerlead others on as they do so.

That said, I would be remiss if I didn't share what I have experienced over my lifetime as a lowly sport trier who is also a curious inquirer and happy observer. Even thinking about the topic is motivating me into that hike this weekend to expand two areas of my brain simultaneously—my motor and auditory cortex—through movement and nature's magical sounds. A brilliant combination.

In the last several decades, the body of research on workout and movement music has swelled considerably, helping psychologists refine their ideas about what makes music such an effective pairing for so many people. It seems that music distracts us from pain and fatigue. But it also elevates our mood and bolsters our endurance, reducing perceived effort. Just ask your friends and family—many will agree that they seem to be able to run farther, bike longer, and swim faster when listening to music.

Over the years, I have spoken at several Running Room stores about the best sort of music for enhancing performance. And yes, although terribly slow, I love joining the classes myself and meeting others like me. I have met many people who are already at the top of their sport and whose goal is to shave two seconds off their best time, and others who are bored with their routine and just want to get started and achieve something. Still others, like me, are looking for a sustainable amount of movement that will keep them healthy as they age—and joyful as they do it.

It all comes back to those goals we discussed earlier. In my talks, I couple much of the information gathered in Track 2 (the science) with stories of what has motivated the hundreds of clients I have worked with—people who require motivation to heal.

Take a minute to contemplate what your movement needs are. In discussing the science of music, I didn't mention that motor functions take up a big part of our brain—we need to develop them in infancy and strengthen them throughout our lives. Movement helps our mood, motivation, and memory—and as we have discussed, so does music. No wonder it makes sense to incorporate the two to fully achieve our goals. If music can help make our movement patterns even more achievable, doesn't that seem like the perfect marriage of positives?

People who exercise seem to have an innate preference for rhythms that are equivalent to 120 beats per minute, or two beats per second. If you were asked to just stand up and begin walking, and to tap your fingers as you did so, chances are you, like most people, would unconsciously settle into a tempo of 120 beats per minute. In an analysis of more than 74,000 popular songs produced between 1960 and 1990, researchers found that the tempo of most—if not all—of them rested at that sweet spot of 120 beats per minute.

While running on the treadmill, though, people tend to favor music of around 160 beats per minute. That seems to be a very comfortable pace for most. So again, you might want to select workout music with a tempo that most accurately matches your desired running pace. If you're more of an elite runner and can do better than a 4.5-minute kilometer or seven-minute mile, then you'll want to pick songs of about 180 beats per minute.

But, like all the good advice and evidence shared throughout this book, it is the personalization of the process and the playlist that keeps you in it to win it—whatever your "it" may be and however you define success.

A few years ago, as I was preparing for a five-kilometer race, I did what I thought I was supposed to do. I looked at the number of beats per minute that I wanted to be able to run, and then picked music with a tempo that I thought was going to challenge me a little bit, but not too much. I put my playlist together, started my run...and found that I had to stop after just two minutes, whereas previously I had been able to run for twenty minutes straight! The tempo of the songs I'd chosen was just too fast for me. I wasn't quite there—yet. Even if the tempo had been a little bit slower, I still would have become quickly exhausted.

After that, I decided to change tacks and put together playlists of the music that most inspired me, regardless of tempo. As a result, I was able to get back to running stronger, and felt better doing it. So, if you're preparing for a race or a sports event and the tempo concept doesn't work for you, try creating a playlist of songs that will trigger your inspiration.

Some people prefer exercising alone; others prefer to have company. However, if exercising on your own makes you feel lonely, listening to familiar music—perhaps tunes that remind you of your friends and the good times you've spent together—can make you feel less alone as you run.

PLAYLISTS TO ACHIEVE YOUR PERSONAL BEST

Here are a few considerations for creating the best playlists to help you achieve your personal best:

Do you want to complete your first race?
Then the playlist you might need for that is "exercise inspiration."

Do you want to improve your cadence?
You're going to want to focus on the rhythm of the music, also known as groove.

Are you looking to improve your power and strength?
It's all about that bass as it will ground you and give you that leverage you want to feel.

Do you want to feel less lonely when you run?
Take familiar music out on the road with you.

▶

It was my eighth week participating in a community running program. The snow had started to fall halfway through the short-distance run. We had just turned down our last street to the finish when it started coming down twice as fast. I stepped off the curb and felt my shoe connect with a slick piece of ice under the new-fallen snow. My ankle buckled and I heard three distinct cracks as I fell to the ground. It was the sound of the end of my new running career.

I remember lying in the snow in the middle of the road and weeping quietly, not just because of the physical pain but because I felt engulfed by a cloud of disappointment. I had wanted to learn to run so badly.

I had decided a few months prior that, if I wanted to avoid living in a nursing home before my time, *now* was the moment to get off the couch and get active. I had seen more than enough research showing the value of just a few intense exercises and some weight-bearing activities each week to get the heart pumping. I had not been doing any of this, and, far from fit and fabulous, was feeling fat and floppy.

After the fall, I found myself back on the couch feeling very sorry for myself. Four months later, after hours of rehab and the soothing words and support of excellent health-care providers and a loving husband, I went back online to look up the next running clinic. That is when I saw it: "triathlon training." I signed up immediately. I couldn't swim, I didn't own a bike, and, well, now you know about my running history. But a feeling of peace came over me with the thought that I would be learning three sports instead of just one. It seemed to somehow better my odds of staying active in at least *one* sport.

Here are the different playlists I put together for when I needed them. I started off with just one playlist, but was surprised to discover that on days I thought I needed a lift, I would turn it on and immediately feel tired, deflated, or just plain off...and I had just started. That was when I realized that the music I had chosen did not match my mood or my needs in those moments. After I expanded to a half-dozen playlists, I was glad I always had a variety of choices of tempo and tone. Please feel free to steal these titles for your needs:

I want to exercise more often—Energy
I want to complete my first race—Motivate
I want to be more productive in my workouts—Momentum
I want to build my confidence and feel strong—Vitality
I want to feel less alone—Nurture
I want to change my outlook on life—Inspiration

I trained hard. I completed my first triathlon. I came in last. I felt sick for two days afterward. But I DID IT—and each one of my playlists absolutely helped me through.

♬

Whether you like classical, death metal, or indie, listening to your own choice of music can improve both your performance and the enjoyment you derive from taking part in competitive sports. Dr. Alexandra Lamont says, "By playing their favorite tunes, we found that participants' exertion levels reduced and their sense of being 'in the zone' increased, when compared to listening to no music at all. The greatest effects were found for music used during training. For those that exercise, music is a way to distract oneself from the physical activity they are enduring and to try to lessen their consciousness of fatigue."

In fact, recent research has found that music does much more than just distract us. Studies conducted by sports psychologists have determined that music has a great impact on the performance level of an athlete. It has been suggested that the correct type of music can heighten an athlete's performance by up to 20 percent. So, whether you are a fan of Bieber or Drake, putting on their latest album could boost your performance and reduce your perceived effort during training and before competing.

♪ **SET YOUR PACE**

Putting together the right playlist for your workouts may simply be a matter of listening to songs on the radio or your favorite streaming service and noticing how your body responds. If whatever you're hearing makes you feel bright and you begin to move automatically, chances are it will spark a similar reaction during your upcoming workout.

Creating the perfect workout playlist is actually really simple. Focus on tempo and what makes you want to groove. The more intense you want the workout to be, the more upbeat the tempo tends to be—but remember, if you are like me and love to feel endurance, a high tempo can also make you feel like you can't keep up.

Here is a list of general tempo guidelines in the exercise world that should help you get started with your workout playlist:

- Yoga, pilates, and other low-intensity activities: 60 to 90 BPM

- Power yoga: 100 to 140 BPM

- CrossFit, indoor cycling, or other forms of HIIT: 140 to 180-plus BPM

- Zumba and dance: 130 to 170 BPM

- Steady-state cardio, such as jogging: 120 to 140 BPM

- Weightlifting and powerlifting: 130 to 150 BPM

- Warming up for exercise: 100 to 140 BPM

- Cooling down after exercise: 60 to 90 BPM

There are many BPM counting apps that can help you find the best music for you that fall in these speeds, as well many pre-made exercise playlists to help you get up and moving. The big streaming services all provide a wide variety of such playlists.

Looking Through the Wellness, Wellplayed Lens

Because music is an intricate blend of sound and silence, what many don't realize is how comforting the very sound of our own breathing can be. If you are feeling overwhelmed, or perhaps feeling extra sensitive to sensory stimulation—if just leaving the house in the morning can feel like a challenge—here is a short exercise to use.

♪ **BREATHE**

That's it. Just Breathe.

The research is clear that three deep breaths can reduce your fight-or-flight response. By breathing more deeply you can break the cycle of panic. Breathing exercises can help reduce tension and relieve stress, thanks to the extra boost of oxygen they give you. While shallow breathing, a marker of stress, stimulates the sympathetic nervous system, deep breathing does the opposite and helps us to calm down.

What's more, breathing exercises have been proven to support the systems that can be harmed by stress. A moment of silence with just deep breathing can reduce blood pressure and may even be able to change the expression of some genes. Everybody has an overwhelm point, though when we reach it is different for each of us. Many of us just keep pushing through the stress, but our goals of accomplishment and productivity become much harder to achieve when we're in this state. With the simple act of pausing wherever you are and taking three deep breathes, you are combating those stress responses and putting your body in a healthier place to better cope with whatever is to come.

We cannot always stay motivated. Motivation comes in spurts. For some people, it lasts; for others, motivation is brief and fleeting. For all of us, navigating the dynamic moments of motivation in our lives means managing the "ups" and balancing them with periods of necessary rest. In my book *Wellness Incorporated*, I talk about creating enough margin so we can manage the inevitable down periods. Margin in motivation does not mean merely managing what you do in a highly motivated state—riding the big wave—it is also about maximizing the moments of rest as you refuel and get ready for the next wave. It is good to know that music, with its many sounds and silences, can be there to help us through it all.

When I started training for the triathlon, riding a bike came back to me quite quickly (it's true that we never forget) and, thanks in part to good coaching, my legs have gotten stronger. Swimming has become a very relaxing, meditative sport—truly a gift for my well-being. Running, for me, continues to be the toughest part. Still a beginner, I find that fast-paced music triggers an impulse to run faster, but ultimately leads to early onset fatigue and overall dissatisfaction with my run. But when I select beloved, moderate, inspirational music, I can continue for a much longer time and feel more positive at the end.

I encourage each of you to experiment with different musical preferences until you find the perfect partner to help your performance. There are very few things that can change a person's feelings in the moment more effectively and quickly than music. And please remember, when jogging alone: It is best NOT to use earbuds/headphones so that you stay aware of your environment. Stay safe and be happy.

OUTRO

Time to Tune In

"Music … can name the unnameable and communicate the unknowable."

LEONARD BERNSTEIN

R EMEMBER, A SONG is never just a song and a playlist is never just a playlist—a song is someone's moment and a playlist is someone's story.

▶

Carrie, a music teacher with decades of experience working in the public school system, now uses music intentionally to support her wellness—but it wasn't always like that.

I had been intimidated to speak to the highly experienced and hugely talented group of music educators that Carrie belonged to, worrying about how receptive they would be to the whole concept of using music intentionally. After the session, Carrie asked if we could speak privately.

We sat with a couple of coffees, and Carrie proceeded to fill me in on the details of her impressive résumé. In addition to leading bands and choirs for years, she had also traveled to Europe on many occasions in her role as a lyric soprano. She loved to perform and conduct, and to teach students. Then she surprised me with this:

"I'm telling you so much of my history, because today I've realized something for the first time: Although I use music daily, I do not use music for myself. I do not use music to intentionally help me through difficult times. In fact, music has become something I share and learn and enjoy, but do not necessarily feed on myself."

Carrie found this subtle change of thinking quite profound. All that she required were a few strategies to bring music into the foreground for her wellness. She began to think about music in a way she had not considered before. She began to document her history with music and all that she had done, but added to that her feelings about it.

▌▌

For the non-musician, the quest of bringing music into the foreground and using it with intention may look different than it did for someone like Carrie. Carrie had all sorts of experience with music and was only lacking the permission she needed to use it in a different way—the way in which *she* wanted to be helped.

Take this book as the permission *you* need to find your music, regardless of your music background, and use it with greater intention to improve your health and well-being. I urge you to take the time, like Carrie did, to document your history with, address your feelings for, and deepen your relationship to music. Go through all the exercises in this book, in your own order and at your own pace.

If I can leave you with just one thought, one key concept, it is this:

Music has the capacity to help you with whatever you are going through. It can truly be your sure friend. Every playlist you develop will bring you into a deep-seeded creative process that will ease your mind and guide you to see your world through a different lens. If you reflect on the past, stay open in the moment, and are willing to embrace the new, your memories, moods, and motivations will continue to grow and change—bringing you a life that is fuller, and more fulfilling, than the life you otherwise would have had.

A life that is truly Wellness, Wellplayed.

Jodi O Photography

AUTHOR BIO

J ENNIFER BUCHANAN'S COMPANY, JB Music Therapy (JBMT), has been instrumental in the implementation of hundreds of music therapy programs throughout Canada since 1991, and has been thrice nominated for the Community Impact Award by the Calgary Chamber of Commerce. There are currently eighteen Certified Music Therapists (MTAs) working at JBMT, serving all ages.

As the author of two award-winning books, *Tune In* and *Wellness Incorporated*, Jennifer has been invited to share her expertise on numerous news and current affairs programs, including NBC, Fox News Health, CBC, iHeart Radio NYC, and CTV, and has been featured in such well-respect publications as *The Guardian*, *Huffington Post*, *The Globe and Mail*, and *Canadian Living*. The Canadian music therapy community has presented her with two lifetime achievement awards: the Frani Award for music therapy advocacy and the Norma Sharpe Award for lifetime achievement.

In addition to being a Certified Music Therapist (MTA), Jennifer delves into music therapy advocacy and policy as the Executive Director of the Canadian Association of Music Therapists. She holds an MBA specializing in social entrepreneurship and speaks at national and international conventions to a wide variety of education, healthcare, government, small business, and corporate audiences.

Jennifer Buchanan lives in Calgary with her husband James, while their two adult children continue to develop their own personal soundtracks, all the while taking turns on what album to put on next.

Find out more at jenniferbuchanan.ca

NOTES

5   *Soon after re-releasing* Tune In *in 2015*, Buchanan, Jennifer (2015), *Tune In: A Music Therapy Approach to Life*. Second Edition. Print. jenniferbuchanan.ca/tune-in-book/

12   *Want a playlist to help your cats relax?*, open.spotify.com/album/4g0YQFz7YWIatmy6EgWGSi

12   *Or try Walk in Like you Own the Place*, huffpost.com/entry/spotify-playlists_n_5695177

12   *the music website and collective Music is my Sanctuary*, musicismysanctuary.com/

12   *"I see building playlists, making mixtapes…,"* see theglobeandmail.com/life/home-and-design/article-why-making-playlists-has-become-a-soothing-pandemic-habit/

13   *the Mixtape Museum (MXM)*, mixtapemuseum.org/

14   *Philips had planned to develop a portable cassette recorder*, see en.wikipedia.org/wiki/Lou_Ottens#Compact_cassette

15   *a great piece of trivia was shared in Ottens' obituary*, see theguardian.com/music/2021/mar/17/lou-ottens-obituary

16   *The CD's unofficial coming out*, see theguardian.com/music/2015/may/28/how-the-compact-disc-lost-its-shine

16   *By 2007, 200 billion CDs had been sold worldwide*, see en.wikipedia.org/wiki/Compact_disc#cite_note-AutoMR-1-2

16   *In his best-selling memoir* Born a Crime, goodreads.com/book/show/29780253-born-a-crime

17   *It all started around 1998*, see lifewire.com/history-of-napster-2438592

18   *like Barack Obama's popular summer set*, see rollingstone.com/music/music-news/barack-obama-summer-playlist-876061/

18   *this little club called Columbia House*, see some of the hilarious ads at retrospace.org/2011/04/retro-fail-24-columbia-record-and-tape.html

19 Popular musicians such as Garth Brooks, from rollingstone.com/music/music-country/
    garth-brooks-weighs-in-on-spotify-controversy-calls-youtube-the-devil-164435/

19 *the two biggest record labels also own the largest streaming service,* see forbes.com/sites/
    benjaminlaker/2020/10/28/heres-how-lockdown-has-shown-that-spotify-has-a-
    sustainability-problem/?sh=793dc538599b

24, *sound information is passed to the auditory cortex and instantaneously broken down,* see
    Deutsch, D. (2010). Hearing music in ensembles. Physics Today, 63(2), 40–45.

25 *and timbre (tone),* Patil, K., Pressnitzer, D., Shamma, S., & Elhilali, M. (2012). Music in
    our ears: The biological bases of musical timbre perception. PLoS Comput Biol 8(11),
    e1002759. doi:10.1371/journal.pcbi.1002759 and Sihvonen, A.J., N. Martinez-Molina,
    and T. Särkämö, Music Perception and Amusia, in Reference Module in Neuroscience
    and Biobehavioral Psychology. 2020. Both references are strong.

25 *stimulating many parts of the brain in both hemispheres,* see Janata, P. Neural basis
    of music perception. Handbook of Clinical Neurology, 2015;129:187–205. doi:
    10.1016/B978-0-444-62630-1.00011-1. PMID: 25726270 (pubmed.ncbi.nlm.nih.
    gov/25726270/)

25 *the heart of our brain's emotional system — the amygdala,* see academic.oup.com/cercor/
    article/17/12/2828/378120

25 *The frontal lobe works in concert with the amygdala,* see Gupta (2011), ncbi.nlm.nih.gov/
    pmc/articles/PMC3032808/

25 *In his best-selling book* Emotional Intelligence, danielgoleman.info/books/
    emotional-intelligence/

26, for more on music and the brain, see:

Prefrontal cortex, Sylvain Moreno (2009) Can Music Influence Language and Cognition?,
    Contemporary Music Review, 28:3, 329–345, DOI: 10.1080/07494460903404410

Motor cortex, Li, G., et al., Identifying enhanced cortico-basal ganglia loops associated
    with prolonged dance training. Scientific Reports, 2015. 5(1): p. 10271, see nature.
    com/articles/srep10271#citeas and Herholz, Sibylle C. and Robert J. Zatorre, Musical
    Training as a Framework for Brain Plasticity: Behavior, Function, and Structure.
    Neuron, 2012. 76(3): p. 486–502

Corpus collosum, Schlaug, G., et al., Increased corpus callosum size in musicians.
    Neuropsychologia, 1995. 33(8): p. 1047–55, see pubmed.ncbi.nlm.nih.gov/8524453/;
    Münte, T.F., E. Altenmüller, and L. Jäncke, The musician's brain as a model of
    neuroplasticity. Nat Rev Neurosci, 2002. 3(6): p. 473–78, see pubmed.ncbi.nlm.nih.
    gov/12042882/, and Steele, C.J., et al., Early Musical Training and White-Matter
    Plasticity in the Corpus Callosum: Evidence for a Sensitive Period. The Journal of
    Neuroscience, 2013. 33(3): p. 1282–90, see jneurosci.org/content/33/3/1282

Amygdala, Hermans, E.J., et al., How the amygdala affects emotional memory by altering
    brain network properties. Neurobiol Learn Mem, 2014. 112: p. 2–16, see pubmed.
    ncbi.nlm.nih.gov/24583373/ and Yang, Y. and J.-Z. Wang, From Structure to Behavior
    in Basolateral Amygdala-Hippocampus Circuits. Frontiers in Neural Circuits, 2017.
    11(86), see frontiersin.org/articles/10.3389/fncir.2017.00086/full

Cerebellum, Nozaradan, S., et al., Specific contributions of basal ganglia and cerebellum to
    the neural tracking of rhythm. Cortex, 2017. 95: p. 156–68, see pubmed.ncbi.nlm.nih.
    gov/28910668/

Sensory cortex, Olszewska, A.M., et al., How Musical Training Shapes the Adult Brain: Predispositions and Neuroplasticity. Frontiers in Neuroscience, 2021. 15(204), see frontiersin.org/articles/10.3389/fnins.2021.630829/full and Borich, M.R., et al., Understanding the role of the primary somatosensory cortex: Opportunities for rehabilitation. Neuropsychologia, 2015. 79(Pt B): p. 246–55, see ncbi.nlm.nih.gov/pmc/articles/PMC4904790/

Auditory cortex, Nelken, I., Music and the Auditory Brain: Where is the Connection? Frontiers in human neuroscience, 2011. 5: p. 106, see ncbi.nlm.nih.gov/pmc/articles/PMC3202228/

Hippocampus, Koelsch, S., Investigating the neural encoding of emotion with music. Neuron, 2018. 98(6): p. 1075–79, see pubmed.ncbi.nlm.nih.gov/29953870/

Visual cortex, Huff, T., N. Mahabadi, and P. Tadi, Neuroanatomy, Visual Cortex, in StatPearls. 2021, StatPearls Publishing. Copyright © 2021, StatPearls Publishing LLC.: Treasure Island (FL), see pubmed.ncbi.nlm.nih.gov/29494110/

27 *As neuroscientist, cognitive psychologist, and best-selling author Daniel Levitin puts it,* see Chanda, Mona Lisa, and Daniel J. Levitin. "The Neurochemistry of Music." Trends in Cognitive Sciences: 179–93; and daniellevitin.com/levitinlab/articles/2013-TICS_1180.pdf

28 *Dr. Randi Hutter Epstein, author of Aroused,* randihutterepstein.com/aroused/

28–9 *Music is widely thought to promote mood stabilization,* see Chanda, Mona Lisa, and Daniel J. Levitin. "The Neurochemistry of Music." Trends in Cognitive Sciences: 179–93.

29 *Dr. Teresa Lesiuk studied music listening,* see journals.sagepub.com/doi/abs/10.1177/0305735605050650

29 *In his research from 2020,* see Front. Hum. Neuroscience, 26 August 2020; doi.org/10.3389/fnhum.2020.00350; and frontiersin.org/articles/10.3389/fnhum.2020.00350/full

29 *Our levels of cortisol,* see Linnemann A, Ditzen B, Strahler J, Doerr JM, Nater UM. "Music listening as a means of stress reduction in daily life." Psychoneuroendocrinology. 2015 Oct;60:82–90. doi: 10.1016/j.psyneuen.2015.06.008. Epub 2015 Jun 21. PMID: 26142566.

29 *music has been found to be just as effective as anti-anxiety medication,* see Berbel P, Moix J, Quintana S. Estudio comparativo de la eficacia de la música frente al diazepam para disminuir la ansiedad prequirúrgica: un ensayo clínico controlado y aleatorizado [Music versus diazepam to reduce preoperative anxiety: a randomized controlled clinical trial]. Rev Esp Anestesiol Reanim. 2007 Jun–Jul;54(6):355–8. Spanish. PMID: 17695946

30 *From as early as in their mother's womb,* see Tan S., Pfordresher P., and Harre R. "Psychology of Music: From Sound of Significance." New York: Psychology Press, 2010 psypress.com/common/sample-chapters/9781841698687.pdf, and Partanen E, Kujala T, Tervaniemi M, Huotilainen M. Prenatal music exposure induces long-term neural effects. PLoS One. 2013;8(10):e78946. Published 2013 Oct 30. doi:10.1371/journal.pone.0078946

30 *There is strong evidence for the connection between stimuli*, see Society For
    Neuroscience. "New Studies Show Factors Responsible For Enhanced Response
    To Music." ScienceDaily, 13 Nov. 2003. Web. 6 Jun 2012. sciencedaily.com/
    releases/2003/11/031113065626.htm; also Mackes, N.K., et al, "Early childhood
    deprivation is associated with alterations in adult brain structure despite subsequent
    environmental enrichment." Proceedings of the National Academy of Sciences, 2020.
    117(1): p. 641–49, and Miendlarzewska, E. A., & Trost, W. J. (2014). How musical
    training affects cognitive development: rhythm, reward and other modulating
    variables. Frontiers in neuroscience, 7, 279. doi.org/10.3389/fnins.2013.00279

32 *most toddlers prefer loud and fast music*, see Lamont A. "Toddlers' musical preferences:
    musical preference and musical memory in the early years." Ann N Y Acad Sci. 2003
    Nov;999:518–19. doi: 10.1196/annals.1284.063. PMID: 14681176.

32 *Multicultural music can enhance the moods of children*, see Dr. Rick Parker semantic
    scholar.org/paper/GEMS-(-Gender-%2C-Education-%2C-Music-%2C-%26-Society-)-
    8-%2C-Parker/17d36c91cb9ab467f92234805a2f7c5889f2c5d7

32 *Like in all things, we grown-ups have an opportunity*, see mic.com/articles/96266/
    there-s-a-magic-age-when-you-find-your-musical-taste-according-to-science

32 *The massive array of "world music" is a great place*, for an introduction, visit worldmusic.
    net/blogs/guide-to-world-music

33 Systematic Review of Music Therapy Practice, see Carr C, Odell-Miller H, Priebe
    S (2013). A Systematic Review of Music Therapy Practice and Outcomes with
    Acute Adult Psychiatric In-Patients. PLoS ONE 8(8): e70252. doi:10.1371/journal.
    pone.0070252

33 *There is evidence that music therapy reduces rates of hospitalization*, see Montánchez
    T.M.L., Juárez R.V., Martínez S.P.C., Alonso G.S., & Torres M, (2016). The benefits of
    using music therapy in mental disorders, omicsonline.org/open-access/benefits-of-
    using-music-therapy-in-mental-disorders-2090-2719-1000116.php?aid=76546

33 *clients of music therapists suffer less anxiety and depression*, see Lee, Jungup & Thyer,
    Bruce A. (2013). Does music therapy improve mental health in adults. Journal of
    Human Behavior in the Social Enviroment, 597–609, and Erkkila, J. , Punkanen,
    M., Fachner, J., Ala-Ruona, E., Po¨ntio¨, I. , Tervaniemi, M., Vanhala, M., & Gold,
    C. (2011). Individual music therapy for depression: randomised controlled trial. The
    British Journal of Psychiatry 199, 132–39.

36 *"Active listening" means that the music is our main focus*, see Peterson, E. (2006).
    Inspired by listening: Teaching your curriculum while actively listening to music:
    Strategies for all teachers. Hampton Falls, NH: Yeogirl Press.

43 *In her book* The Success–Energy Equation, see michellecederberg.com/books/

46 *the Canadian Hard of Hearing Association*, to learn more visit chha.ca/

46 *High-volume, risk-associated behaviors can permanently damage*, see who.int/pbd/
    deafness/activities/MLS_Brochure_English_lowres_for_web.pdf

49 *Dr. Laurel Young, a music therapist researcher*, see Young, L. (2020). Challenging
    assumptions about aging, dementia, and how music helps. Music Therapy Today,
    16(1), 199–200. Available online: issuu.com/presidentwfmt/docs/mtt._vol._16._n_1;
    Hebblethwaite, S., Young, L., & Martin-Rubio, T. (2020). Pandemic precarity: Aging

and social engagement. Leisure Sciences. DOI: 10.1080/01490400.2020.1773998, and Young, L. (2017, February 11). Challenging assumptions about how music helps, blog post forOxford University Press available at blog.oup.com/2017/02/challenging-assumptions-how-music-helps/

50 *In early 2021, an incredible list of artists*, see the original letter at musiciansunion.org.uk/news/calling-on-the-pm-to-put-the-value-of-music-back-in-the-hands-of-music-makers%E2%80%9D, and a discussion of the parliamentary report at bbc.com/news/entertainment-arts-57838473?fbclid=IwAR0Ie07fTbYHKsE2J0daKuZj3RcDV4nQeuz9r6YIbGfcbHaS2l2f3sfxKVw

52 *surveys show it's in fact millennial consumers driving the vinyl revival*, see themanual.com/culture/why-vinyl-is-coming-back/

54 *governments addressing the "digital divide,"* see policyresponse.ca/the-digital-divide-is-about-equity-not-infrastructure/

59 *"What seems to happen is that a piece of familiar music...,"* see ucdavis.edu/search/news_detail.lasso?id=9008

59 *Research suggests that most people stop adding new music to their personal soundtrack*, see businessinsider.com/why-we-stop-discovering-new-music-around-age-30-2018-6

65 *The brain undergoes rapid neural development during the first years of life*, see Casey B.J., Tottenham N., Liston C., Durston S. "Imaging the developing brain: what have we learned about cognitive development?" Trends in Cognitive Sciences 9.3 (March 2005): 104–10. sciencedirect.com/science/article/pii/S1364661305000306

66 *Our ears become attuned to certain styles and textures*, see Levitin, Daniel J. *This is Your Brain on Music: The Science of a Human Obsession.* New York: Dutton/Penguin, 2006. penguinrandomhouse.com/books/298964/this-is-your-brain-on-music-by-daniel-j-levitin/

67 *music seems to be intrinsically linked to our forming of our personal identity*, see journals.sagepub.com/doi/10.1177/2059204320965058

68 *music seems to be associated with positive emotional memories with social themes*, see journals.sagepub.com/doi/10.1177/0305735619888803

72 *However, under the right circumstances, all music is retrievable*, see Williamon A. & Egner T. "Memory structures for encoding and retrieving a piece of music: an ERP investigation." Cognitive Brain Research, 22: 36–44, available at lib.bioinfo.pl/paper:15561499

77 "Sound of Silence Activates Auditory Cortex," see nature.com/articles/434158a

78 *"Music often accompanies emotional events,"* see abc.net.au/news/2020-06-27/music-memory-song-that-takes-you-back-to-a-moment-in-time/12391160#:~:text=%22Music%20often%20accompanies%20emotional%20events,itself%20is%20an%20emotional%20thing%20%E2%80%A6

82 *Listening to inspiring music and engaging in discussions*, see sciencedaily.com/releases/2017/05/170524101507.htm

84 *Some research suggests that listening to music that soothes is as effective as taking 10 mg of valium*, see pubmed.ncbi.nlm.nih.gov/17695946/

90 *according to recent research from Durham University in the United Kingdom*, see dur.ac.uk/news/newsitem/?itemno=28329

136   *Wellness, Wellplayed*

90 *A 2013 study in* The Journal of Positive Psychology, see tandfonline.com/doi/abs/10.10 80/17439760.2012.747000

96 *Research shows that listening to music can definitely lift your mood*, see healthline.com/ health-news/mental-listening-to-music-lifts-or-reinforces-mood-051713#Music-as-therapy

96–97 *For example, a memorable hallucination of a dancing "baby,"* see hollywoodreporter.com/ movies/movie-news/hollywood-flashback-ally-mcbeal-made-meme-history-a-dancing-baby-1998-1027243/

103 *In her book* The Power of Music, *Elena Manne*s, see Mannes, Elena. The Power of Music: Pioneering Discoveries in the New Science of Song. New York: Walker &, 2011. More at npr.org/2011/06/01/136859090/the-power-of-music-to-affect-the-brain

104 *In 1959, a doctor named H.R. Teirich*, see Teirich, H.R. (1959). "On therapeutics through music and vibrations." In Scherchen, H. (ed.), *Gravesaner Blatter*. Mainz: Ars Viva Verlag

106 *I worked with personal branding expert Leela Jacobs*, visit her at leelajacobs.com

108 *In a study of 36,000 participants from around the world,* see verywellmind.com/music-and-personality-2795424 (the actual article is linked inside this one).

111 *In a study commissioned by the UK licensing organizations,* see bloomberg.com/news/ articles/2012-06-29/music-boosts-workplace-productivity-licensers-claim

112 *According to Dr. Teresa Lesiuk*, see journals.sagepub.com/doi/ abs/10.1177/0305735605050650

114 *In an analysis of more than 74,000 popular songs*, see scientificamerican.com/article/ psychology-workout-music/

118 *Whether you like classical, death metal, or indie*, see sciencedaily.com/ releases/2012/04/120417221709.htm

118 *Studies conducted by sports psychologists*, see serendipstudio.org/exchange/gflaherty/ effects-music-athletic-performance

119 *Here is a list of general tempo guidelines*, see more at cnet.com/health/fitness/ how-to-create-the-perfect-workout-playlist/

ACKNOWLEDGMENTS

COULD NOT HAVE surrounded myself with a better team to produce this book. First and foremost, my extraordinary editor, Scott Steedman; from the moment we met, you got it!! You helped me fulfill the purpose of this book—to engage music lovers, ignite memories, and bring more meaning to people's lives with music. Jennifer Lum, your design is truly a work of art that captures the essence of this book; thank you. I would not have met these incredible people if it wasn't for Jesse Finkelstein and the Page Two team, who I am so honored to be identified with as one of their authors.

During the preparation of *Wellness, Wellplayed* I found insights and accuracy with the help of Julie Joyce, scientific consultant, and Linda Doughty, who helped me organize my thoughts as I developed new stories and concepts. Also thanks to the talented Lisa Jacobs, musician and music therapist, and Felicia Lifton, my brilliant niece, both of whom read the first draft and shared their skilled and valuable feedback. My favorite comment from Felicia, age eighteen, was, "What's a Napster?" That made me realize that my precious music history was already being forgotten by the next generation. This book aims to change that—and yes, "a Napster" is now more accurately defined.

And finally, thank you to my dear friend Michelle Oucharek-Deo, who meets me every Saturday morning to reminisce about our lives' soundtracks and the many more songs we have yet to play.

Made in the USA
Columbia, SC
27 September 2021

45596064R00093